Getting to Know You

Getting To Know You

A Guide to Communicating

by

Marjorie Umphrey

Harvest House Publishers
Irvine, California 92714

GETTING TO KNOW YOU

Copyright © 1976 Harvest House Publishers
Irvine, California 92714
Library of Congress Catalog Card Number: 76-21982
ISBN-0-89081-025-7

Printed in the United States of America

Acknowledgements

I wish to extend my appreciation to:

My secretary, Debra Maurice, who worked diligently on the typing of this manuscript.

Ron Hallaian and Hallaian and Associates who gave direction to my dreams.

Contents

Silence Became My Instructor

I had always assumed that I was above average in the art of communicating. I was a public school teacher, mother of three and I enjoyed being with people. As I started that particular school year, little did I know what would happen to me by the time my class of second graders moved on to the third grade.

School was well into the semester and I was loving every minute of it. How lucky could anyone be? My education was behind me. I was making a living teaching an adorable bunch of second graders in an excellent school district in Southern California. What more could I ask for in life?

My only complaint was a hoarse voice. Some days by lunch time, the children were complaining that they couldn't hear me. "You sound funny, teacher," was a phrase I heard over and over again. Teachers do get tired voices, and with that thought, the problem was dismissed. It was a professional hassle I would simply have to accept. But the coarse tones soon turned into whispers.

Believe it or not, I taught several months with the aid of a transistor mike. The classroom started to take on the character of a theater in the round and sometimes must have even appeared to be a 3-ring circus. But the kids loved it and enjoyed learning with their "whispering teacher."

After examinations and tests by several physicians, the verdict was papillomas of the vocal chords—not vocal misuse. That meant surgery. "So what," I thought. "What's a little surgery on my vocal chords. In a month I'll be back with my second graders."

I went back to my classroom—but not in a month and not to my children. Four months later I entered an empty room late in the evening. I had to go through my desk and pack up all my teaching materials. I put my head down on the desk that was no longer mine and cried. I'm not sure why I cried. It could have been because I was in love with a bunch of kids with whom I could no longer play and exchange ideas. Or, I could have been angry that after wading through all that education, I would lose the great job I had. I suppose I was questioning and accusing God for allowing this to happen to me. I'm certain, however, that most of my tears were a reaction to a quiet, subtle fear that I'd never again regain full use of my voice.

What was to be one minor bit of surgery turned into four years of silence and six surgeries.

The Winter of My Life

The person I am now is a total stranger to the person I use to be. When I try to look back and relate to the "me" of the past, I draw a blank. I mean this quite literally. Those days were the winter of my life. Today, I really feel like spring with all its newness and vitality. There's a certain boldness to spring. The colors in nature are distinct and vivid. Springtime seems right to us, and we often are more aware of life and enjoy living it. There are no springs, however, without the winters. From death comes new life. For this reason, I can never regret the winter that I experienced. Out of my despair came hope. Out of my shame came reality.

That period of my life was terribly unhappy. Perhaps the one word that sums it all up to me now is "emptiness." You see, had I really known myself previously, I would have had the strength I needed. Instead, I experienced confusion!

What about my faith in God, you ask. To be honest, that simply added to the confusion. Don't get me wrong. God was not confusing me. He was precious and caring all the while. I was the mixed up one! Because I had never gotten to know me and settle so many issues of life, the loss of my voice threw me into a state of crisis. I had no inner resources to draw upon and couldn't seem to reach out to God as a resource. I suppose in retrospect, I wanted to blame God for the whole thing.

From as young as I can remember I had received strong injunctions from my parents to (1) not feel and

(2) not be close. If I had feelings, I was to camouflage them and definitely not show them. I continually received double messages on the idea of closeness. Theoretically, good families were to be close, but in reality, there was no touching and no show of emotion.

Along with this, I was expected to be perfect and work like crazy for anything and everyone. I was taught well. Any idea of reaching out for help was automatically discounted in my head.

Can you see where I was?

1. No inner resources.
2. Unable to allow myself feeling or the expression of that feeling.
3. Unable to be close.
4. Unable to reach out.
5. Rejecting of God.

The result—Chaos! Without boring you with details, I was an angry person who couldn't and wouldn't show it. Did I feel desperate? Oh, yes! Did I want to take my life? Certainly! Why not? It seemed like the only honorable thing to do. My background told me that it was not okay to feel or express my feelings. The only way to experience relief and not hurt anyone or violate what I had been taught was to vanish away.

Why am I telling you all this? To give you HOPE. There's no problem or condition too difficult to overcome. I've had people say to me after a workshop, "I'd give anything to be like you, or have your knowledge and experience." I always smile and say gently, "would you?"

Hope is always available and I want you to believe

and accept that for you. The solutions are not always easy. Time, dedication, determination and work go into getting where you want to go. The steps that worked for me were:

1. I reached bottom.
2. I *decided* to live.
3. That decision to live did not mean mere existence—I decided to really live.
4. I reaffirmed my faith in the Lord and asked for His best.
5. I took full responsibility for me and my place in life (I stopped blaming).
6. I took time out to get to know me.
7. I refused to look back.
8. I set small goals and gradually added to my list.
9. I have gotten to know and like myself.
10. I have a positive attitude.

I couldn't remain a recluse for four years. It's important for you to understand that while I was in silence, I was not in solitude. I was with people! But being with people didn't help the loneliness, the depression and the loss. To be honest, I felt like a vegetable. What contribution could I make to others without a voice? The reversal of that question rang out also—what contribution was anyone making to me now that I had no voice?

So I sat—sat in restaurants, classrooms, churches, parties and observed. What else was there to do but observe? What I saw changed me. I was appalled at the total inability of human beings to relate to one another. I was angry that in many cases people didn't even seem to care if they communicated. I was sad that so many precious moments were being lost by people. I was frightened over the blatant disregard for feelings. But this was the beginning of communication for me.

Some of the most obvious and most common errors in communication were:

1. Interrupting another person.
2. No interest in what the other is saying.
3. Parental and judgmental attitudes.
4. Argumentation.
5. Poor eye contact.
6. Insensitivity.
7. Talking about self too much.
8. Disregard for feelings (embarrassing the other party).
9. Monopolizing the conversation.
10. Discounting the other person.

I discovered very quickly that the majority of people were on some sort of soap box. They had a "cause" and every conversation was an opportunity to further that cause. The rest of the people seemed too frightened to talk with anyone.

When I was having dinner with four to six people at a restaurant, the most apparent problem was lack of interest. Someone would be talking and others would discount him. By this I mean, they would talk among themselves, or their eyes would wander off making it obvious they weren't listening.

I have gone to dinner many times and not be given the opportunity to speak in a two-hour span. When I could only whisper, I'd write on a magic slate and pass it around. Can you imagine the impact my comment made. (I say that with tongue in cheek.) Since my voice returned, I have still been in situations where I was not given the opportunity to speak. I have learned, however, to make an opportunity.

If you were to ask me what was the worse situation I observed, I would have to say the comments between family members. On countless occasions, I found myself extremely uncomfortable when family members would: (1) play all kinds of psychological games, (2) engage in an outright war, (3) talk about intimate subjects around mere acquaintances, (4) be discourteous to each other, (5) discount their partner or child verbally.

On one occasion, a couple was playing a game with another couple. The husband didn't agree with a move his wife made. He said, "You're so stupid! That was so dumb! What's the use in even playing. I'll never be your partner again!" The woman ran from the room in tears. At this point, I was angry also. My mind was made up. This kind of "fun" isn't worth it. I've never been with this man socially again.

My husband and I met a very distinguished gentleman for lunch one afternoon. I was delighted in that I didn't know him very well, but had heard he was a very interesting person. We exchanged a few social phrases and ordered lunch. At this point, the man turned his chair from me and faced my husband. The conversation continued between the two of them. Occasionally, I tried to add to the subject, but got no response. In 1½ hours, the man never addressed his remarks to me. I left that day feeling "ripped-off."

Many more illustrations will follow in this book. There is enough evidence, I hope, to make it clear to you that:

1. People are talking, but not saying anything.

2. They are hearing, but not actively listening.

3. They often do not even look at one another.

4. When they look, they don't see the distress and cries for help.

Most important of all, there seems to be a sick lack of desire to feel and care for others and even for ourself.

What About The Springtime?

As I mentioned earlier, I am a total stranger to the person I used to be. At this point in my life, it is both unnecessary and impossible for me to look back and know the woman of years ago. Ah yes, there are still those who would want me to look back, but I don't!

I liken this part of my life to spring because I feel so very much alive. *I'm* alive. I'm not living for some organization. Before, I sought to please everyone which is quite a box to put yourself into.

There's a boldness to spring, and I have a new

boldness. I've dealt with most of my fears, and I now approach each day with a new confidence. I also have the confidence that God knows and loves me unconditionally. I approach Him as a loving, caring Father and friend.

The colors in nature are vivid and distinct during springtime. During those days of winter, I was never distinct or glowing with happiness. I was a puppet performing at the request of relatives, friends or church people. Now that I am congruent with self, I'm comfortable and that happiness and peace shines through. I'm not suggesting that everyone likes me or what I do. This is no magic solution for instant friendship. What I am saying is that I now like myself and I am one with God and with me. This brings peace and security even when trouble or criticisms come.

We usually feel right and good in the spring. We're motivated to do new projects. We feel good about life. That sums it up for me. I'm swamped with work. I've had terrible disappointments this year. I've had difficult tasks to complete. Still, I can say with all the honesty I possess, I feel right and good about myself.

I want so much for this book to change your life. There is hope. There is a springtime for you. It is time for you to learn to communicate.

Barriers to Communication

When we approach the problem of communication, we attack the root of many other problems. I am convinced that ineffective communication is the basis for all problems in relationships. I am not suggesting that if you can effectively communicate you will be problem free. What I am suggesting is that with effective communication, you will be able to work through all problems. I believe effective communication is preventative medicine. How many future problems could you avoid through honest, loving communication?

Communication Defined

The dictionary defines communication as (1) transmitting, (2) a giving and exchange of information, (3) a message. How would you define communication?

Be careful not to generalize too much as to your definition of communication. That's a primary reason why there is so much discussion on the subject and so little application.

The meaning of the term *communication* may be unclear to you. Go a step further. Is the depth of the term *communication* clear to you? If communication is mere talking, we are all handicapped in developing relationships. In my exploration of the depth and totality of communication, I define communication as the following:

1. Communication is giving and receiving a message.
2. Communication is giving of oneself.
3. Communication is receiving part of someone else.
4. Communication is sharing ideas, feelings and moments with another person.
5. Communication is experiencing another human being.
6. Communication is the giving and receiving of an emotional stroke.
7. Communication is getting my needs met.
8. Communication is meeting another person's needs.
9. Communication is looking at and seeing what another person is saying.
10. Communication is listening and hearing what others are saying.
11. Communication is my face and body talking.

12. Communication is using all my senses to recognize what the other's face and body and voice is saying.
13. Communication is putting myself in the other's place.
14. Communication is touching.
15. Communication is reaching out.
16. Communication is tenderness and caressing.
17. Communication is words on the printed page.
18. Communication is allowing someone else to intrude into your world of thoughts.
19. Communication is expression through the arts.
20. Communication is spiritual.

Barriers to Communication

There are many barriers to effective communication. These barriers must be approached and hurdled in order to develop satisfying relationships with others. That's what we mean when we say we want to communicate.

The art of communicating is not relating to inanimate objects, or nature, but to other human beings. Communication is one human being relating to another. This is a basic emotional need—to love and to be loved by others—to express ourselves to others and to have our needs met by experiencing good one-to-one relationships.

Since there are so many barriers, I am going to discuss the ones I feel to be the most obvious and the most damaging.

1. *You*

You are the first barrier that can get in the way. You may not want to relate to others. People sit in my office every week and describe to me their need to develop more one-to-one relationships. Yet, no positive results occur because they have not made the decision to *want* to relate. For whatever reason or reasons that may exist for this lack of desire, you must make up your mind to want relationships.

2. *Fear*

Fear is probably the most damaging of all the barriers. Fear locks the doors to so many opportunities and robs us of beautiful relationships. Some of our most common areas of fear are:

Fear of Rejection. This is always the first fear that is named by the people involved in my seminars and workshops. When I ask them to discuss this fear, I can see the significance of the problem by the passion of their answers and the expression on their faces as they often will say, "I'd rather be by myself and experience loneliness than risk rejection." I remember so well when this subject came up while conducting a Transactional Analysis group. After about twenty minutes of discussion, the group realized that every one of them were lonely and craving for a one-to-one relationship. Still, none of them would have ever tried to communicate with the other had it not been for their particular climate of group therapy. It was so frightening and so sad that several people wanted to talk more about why they were so afraid to communicate. They began to fantasize about how many people scattered all over Los Angeles and across the country have similar needs that will not be met because of the fear of rejection.

Some typical statements that I have heard regarding this fear of rejection are:

1. "I don't want to talk to anyone that I don't know, whether they like me or not."
2. "What if he doesn't want to talk to me?"
3. "I've been hurt so many times I can't risk another one."
4. "I've never had love returned. Why should I give it?"
5. "I couldn't face rejection."
6. "People usually like everyone but me."

Fear of Involvement. Have you ever said to yourself while listening to a conversation, "I'm really not interested in getting involved with that person." Perhaps you are thinking that you might like him, but just don't want to start a friendship. This could be based on bad experiences in the past, other fears, the inability to trust others or even a lack of time. You can easily see the vicious cycle that can occur: You fear involvement (building a relationship, intimacy, friendship) so you refuse to get involved in the conversation. The lack of communication inhibits the possibility of future relationships. The lack of relationships produces a stronger feeling of loneliness and rejection. The cycle goes on and on and soon becomes a way of life.

A man said to me not so long ago, "I don't talk much to people because I don't like to get involved." I asked him to define involvement. At this point, he became more direct and said, "Well, I may never see most people I meet again (much less become friends with them) so what good is it to even start a conversation. It seems to me to be a waste of time."

If you have felt this way, may I suggest some thoughts:

1. See every person as having something he or she can contribute to you.

2. Think of every person and situation as an experience. These experiences add color and flavor to your existence.

3. When you meet and talk to someone casually, consider the possibility that you could be a positive factor, a moment of happiness or an ambassador of hope to them.

4. Be aware that every encounter with people is a growth process.

5. Reflect on your dearest friends—another "angel unaware" could come into your life if you conquer this fear of involvement.

Fear of Responsibility. Closely related to the fear of involvement is the fear of responsibility. "I want to be responsible for me and no one else . . ." "I can't handle what's going on in my own head—how can I relate to others." "No one cares about me, why should I care about them." "You do your thing and I'll do mine." These are fairly common statements made by those who fear responsibility.

When you build a relationship it does require responsibility, but that can be determined by the individuals involved. Effective communication doesn't always call for an excessive amount of responsibility on your part or others. Naturally, some people with whom you communicate will be extremely significant to you—your family, close friends or children. To these people you will experience a definite sense of responsibility. There is no reason, however, why you can't engage in some forms of good communication without having to make that type of a commitment.

For myself, I can think of people who are close, dear friends of mine but I seldom see them. We are secure in one another and we each know that should the other be in need that we'd be there to help. Then too, there are many people I chat with during the week and enjoy, but towards whom I feel no commitment to a high level of involvement. Even now, as I reflect on this, I'm happy that I've been able to experience all of these people. This could not have been possible had I let my fears rule them out.

Fear To Risk Vulnerability. We fear revealing ourselves. We might also say we fear revealing our fears.

When I expose myself to you, I am actually giving you some power over me. I'm now vulnerable. When I become vulnerable, I need feedback from you and reassurance.

Do you remember when you fell in love, I mean *really* fell in love? When you finally realized it and expressed it openly to your lover, you became extremely vulnerable. All your feelings were exposed, and you experience the other person as having a great deal of power over you. The passion of love was at this point both beautiful and painful. You were afraid of losing your new love, and you constantly wanted to care and experience caring in return.

In other areas of life we are afraid to reveal ourselves. Rather than risk being known, we play roles. We throw up some barriers, put on a mask and build a tight case against our fears and what is buried beneath the surface.

"If I don't talk, no one can find me out," is a statement often said to me in counseling.

I find this fear especially strong in ministers and their families. Quite naturally they want to set examples and they feel that parishioners and others expect strength and control at all times. Yet, they often wrestle with needs, cares, physical problems, financial worries, and other situations common to man. The idea of revealing their fears, temptations and cares to anyone is so overwhelming that they often play a role. This role is a blend between God, the Apostle Paul and a modern day computer. Unfortunately, sometimes the person actually comes to believe this role he is playing. In other words, he assumes all of these God-like qualities to the point of denying his own needs and feelings. Because he is not deity, he hurls upon himself an unrealistic challenge which destines him to inevitable defeat. To this person, the defeat is usually more dramatic, more severe and more damaging than to others.

I'd like to share with you a little about my own life. Being a minister's wife was an exciting challenge to me. I was called to serve the Lord long before I was married. It didn't take long, however, until I became aware that much of what was expected of me was incongruent with what I felt within myself. The pressures to conform and to perform produced a lot of guilt within me. I continued to press on, denying my own inadequacies and expecting near perfection. My drives to please all and to accomplish perfection led to discouragement, a great deal of anger and ultimately to failure. I remember thinking on many occasions how I hated the words, "Margie can do it." I was dying to say, "No, I can't—and I won't!" Finally, the passion of my soul was to prove to all the world my own unworthiness so they would never expect anything of me again.

Communication involves dealing with this fear barrier. Willingness to risk "being known" will build relationships based on truth rather than a role played by a confused actor.

3. *Distrust Is A Common Barrier*

I can't count the number of times people have said to me, "I trust no one!" There could well be many causes for this distrust; however, the ability to trust is needed in building effective communication.

Society perpetuates a philosophy of insecurity, doubt and distrust. Our own country has suffered greatly in the last few years in this area. Citizens are doubting their country's leadership, children experience little or no security at home, adolescents refuse to communicate with parents because of distrust, and a man's word is no longer held as good.

This total attitude of distrust can generate a negative type of personality. If I refuse to trust anyone with whom I come in contact, my attitude toward people and life will have a negative slant. What in life can be beautiful if it is tainted with suspicion? I knew an extremely handsome intellectual man who knew and loved the Lord. His life had not been easy and stress had caused a build-up of distrust. At one point in his life even God came under attack. He gradually became comfortable in a victim position and indulged himself in playing the "Poor Me" game. He began every venture and approached all relationships with a question mark. He was defeated before he began.

We go back to the concept in Transactional Analysis that suggests that the healthy way to view life is: "I'm okay, you're okay." Personally, I can't imagine myself thinking that I'm the only one who can be trusted. Realistically, I must accept the fact that I need relationships. I need to interact with people. I must trust others. This need can energize in me a desire to see others from more loving and trusting eyes.

4. *Shyness and Inhibitions*

All of us start off in life a little on the shy side. We like to be around our close friends and function in a secure environment. New faces and new surroundings are often threatening and we back off. We classify this behavior as being shy. Usually, a wise, understanding parent and an alert, helpful teacher can help children work out these problems of shyness. When we work out these shy feelings through life, communicating becomes easier and easier.

The opposite occurs when the problem of shyness remains unresolved. Rather than building positive experiences, the feelings intensify and we become withdrawn and inhibited. I know of men and women who have chosen to be inhibited and now relate to inanimate objects rather than to other human beings. Some withdraw into music and art. They can't seem to join the group or enjoy another person. Crowds are frightening and socialization is next to zero.

When this type of person reaches adulthood, life is a mere cloud of hurt, rejection and failure. You can see immediately that very few, if any, opportunities for success in relationships, love and fulfillment could become a reality.

If you experience yourself as shy or inhibited, try these suggestions:

1. Question yourself as to whether or not you are genuinely shy or inhibited. You may think you are and feel you are—but are you? Here's why I ask . . .

2. Ask yourself whether or not you learned to be shy in order to get various types of strokes (recognition) or to avoid certain unpleasant situations or responsibilities.

3. Seek out a professional counselor or psychologist who can properly test you out on the problem.

4. Pursue counseling if the problem exists and is a barrier to communication.

5. *Internalized Feelings*

We sometimes have barriers within our own mind and thoughts about ourselves that hinder our communication. Sometimes these attitudes and perceptions came from our parents or some other authority figures. For various reasons, we develop some feelings about ourselves, and these internalized feelings effect what we do and say to others.

For example, bad feelings about your own body and appearance will prevent you from socializing. You may experience yourself as overweight and unappealing. This fantasy about yourself will lead you to compare your appearance with other members of your sex. Feelings of inadequacy soon grow to the point where we find ourselves withdrawing. We have little to say because of our feeling of inferiority.

You may perceive yourself as "stupid" or lacking in the ability to think. Perhaps you wouldn't label yourself as so, but you behave as such. You don't value your own opinion. You are constantly deferring to others even when you believe your ideas to be correct. Decision making is difficult for you. You would prefer that someone else make up your mind for you. There is a constant need for assurance and approval even in the smallest ventures.

I often have a woman confide to me that she doesn't experience herself as feminine. I've heard these words from both single and married women. It doesn't seem to matter how many physical assets she may have in her favor. She feels unfeminine and this internalized feeling stirs up negative results in communication. This opinion might have come from early childhood. Dad might have wanted a boy and so he treated her like one. Unfortunate teenage years with little socialization could still be giving her problems. Of course, if the woman is married or deeply involved with a man, he is a factor in her opinion of herself.

I'm sure, by now, ideas are flashing through your head about you. You're probably getting in touch with some internalized feelings that have been barriers to your communication.

Here are some exercises and suggestions that will help you eliminate internalized feelings that serve as barriers to you.

1. *Recognize What They Are*. This calls for honest evaluation on your part. Name them, write them down, discuss them. Do what you must to recognize them enough to want to do something about them.

2. *Consider the Facts*. Use your senses and your own intelligence to look at yourself. Evaluate yourself from a purely intellectual level. Weigh the facts. Make a list of your obvious assets.

3. *Ask The Opinion of Others*. I'm sure you have friends and acquaintances whose opinion you value. Tell them about your internalized feelings and ask them to frankly and honestly express how they perceive you. Listen to what they say. If you value their judgments and opinions on other subjects, you should also accept as valid their perceptions of you.

4. *Practice Constructive Self Doubt*. This is directly associated with the ideas in number 3. When a friend or counselor expresses his positive opinion of you, practice doubting your feelings rather than what is being said to you. You can also doubt that your judgments are always right.

   Some years ago a lovely young woman came to my office complaining of a low self-image. She reported to me that she was unable to attract a man because of her unattractive appearance. It didn't take a second glance to convince me of the woman's obvious beauty. After becoming more familiar with her I explained to her that I experienced her as being very attractive. She immediately began to protest my compliments, and at this point a "game" could easily have been initiated.

   The therapy that followed centered around the omnipotent qualities she was assigning to herself. In other words, her ideas and words were all that were valid. What I said as a professional had no credability. What her friends said meant nothing. Her persistence to hold on to this negative view of herself validated to me that she held herself to be somewhat God-like. This led her to a great deal of pain and defeat. She quickly saw that God-like qualities should not do that, but rather cause us to feel good about ourselves.

6. *Depression and Anxiety*

We have all experienced anxiety and depression. You no doubt can remember quite vividly the hurt involved.

Exactly what is depression? Depression is a condition of human experience. Depression cuts across all human behavior ranging from severe problems to everyday experiences when we suffer loss. Depression is a conscious feeling of hopelessness and despair. It is a condition of human experience, and has many causes.

There is a positive side to depression. If I am unable to feel depression, I also would be unable to feel love. The depression can be a reflection of real caring.

Another positive aspect of depression is its motivating effect to reach out for other relationships. If I'm experiencing a great burden of depression, I probably will feel a tremendous loneliness and emptiness. This pain is what can activate the ability to reach out and say, "I'm needy . . . please help me." Before this I may not have realized my need for others and their emotional support. Or if I had known it, I might not have been willing to admit it. The depression, however, brought enough pain to push me into a move towards people.

What about the part of depression that serves as a barrier to communication? Depression interferes with communication when we are feeling a lot of despair. We don't believe that anyone cares about us or will listen to us. There is no one who will do anything to help or can do anything to help. We push all of these feelings down inside of us. They grow and grow. This shows itself when there is nothing inside of us that will rally us to reach for help. There are no internal resources that can make us bounce back. We withdraw from everyone. This is the angry side of us. We are really saying through our withdrawal, "The world has brought me pain."

Perhaps the following suggestions will help you if depression is a barrier to your communication.

1. Understand that you have been terribly hurt and experienced a loss (loss of love, employment, age, health, etc.).

2. Understand that nothing can replace that loss.

3. Accept that there are other avenues to explore that can act as a substitute and relieve you of some of the pain.

4. Believe the promise that God always gives us a way out.

5. Take one small step towards people and relationships. Give yourself an opportunity to experience yourself and the outside slowly.

Which of these barriers keep you from communicating? You may even want to make a list of your own of other barriers. The issue here is that you recognize the barriers for what they are and for the harm they can do. Your awareness of the barriers and your willingness to remove them will thrust you way ahead in the art of communication.

Are You Talking to Yourself?

Where do you begin? You begin with you! That's right—you are the most important part of communication. It all begins with you getting acquainted with you.

You may laugh at this or think it's silly. Some of you are probably throwing up your hands and saying to yourself, "If I'm going to have to go to all that trouble, forget it!" Hold on for a second—it may not be so bad or even much trouble. The whole project can even be fun.

There's a lot more emphasis on self-awareness today. This is a super asset for our young people. Of course, many don't pay any attention to it, but still, the opportunity is available.

To those of you who are thirty and above, this idea may seem uncomfortable to you. I'm quite sure, however, that you continually wish that you had been given a more open invitation in your youth to look at yourself. Men and women come to my office every day expressing regrets for the past. More often, their regrets center around a lack of freedom in the past to explore self. Some express these resentments directly with steaming hostility. Usually, the pains only appear in mild overtones—but they are there—in the rich and poor, the Christian and the non-Christian. They all seem to be asking, "Why didn't society give our generation permission to know ourselves better and be the best of that discovery?"

Why live in regrets? Why delay communication because it might cost you a little time and effort? Anything worth having takes going after it.

How do you start? That depends on where you are right now in your own experience. Some of you younger citizens are fairly well tuned in to you, your needs, your feelings, your goals. If you're not, take note right now that all kinds of help is available to you. To those of you who are breaking out of your old mold for the first time in thirty, forty, fifty years, you can expect more work. For you, it will take courage. Any change will bring a certain amount of fear. Admit your fear—it's okay—but don't let it stop you from talking to yourself.

Talking to yourself begins with evaluation. Very seldom does anyone come to my office when a problem symptom first shows itself. The majority of people wait until it's almost too late. Those of us in the counseling field usually find ourselves dealing with crisis situations.

If businesses and institutions waited as long as individuals and families did to evaluate themselves, the economic trends would be extremely depressing.

You know some of the more common rationalizations, don't you?

"I don't want to change!"

"I'm too old to change!"

"This is the way I've always been, so why change now?"

"People will just have to take me the way I am."

"What if I do change, and people don't like the new me?"

"I'm afraid to get to know the real me—I'm afraid of what I might find."

"I don't have the courage to change—even if I wanted to."

"I've done a good job of fooling people all these years—I can't stop now."

"I would disappoint my family if I revealed my true self."

"All my responsibilities don't allow me the luxury of self discovery."

What have been some of your excuses? Some of your unconscious reasons have come from your parents, your culture and your religion. Regardless of their origin, we build up certain defenses that block self-evaluation and disclosure.

Let me share with you some of the problems I encountered in learning to know myself.

I grew up in a rigid environment. I was the only child and discipline was strong. A great deal of my childhood still remains fuzzy to me. One thing still is vivid to me—there was one way to do everything and we always did everything the same way. Life was scheduled to the smallest point, and nothing ever threw that schedule off.

I can't remember any gray areas in my life. You know what I mean—every word, thought, feeling or behavior was either black or white, good or bad, right or wrong. There never seemed to be any options in life.

This is what I meant by a rigid sort of environment. I received my recognition by performing up to the standard expected of me. I quickly learned to *adapt* to whatever was necessary in order to keep peace and receive positive rewards. I remember one day when I was only about eight, I was playing with some of the neighborhood children. An argument began, and I quietly and quickly acquiesced to the others. Later, my mother scolded me for giving in, and made this statement, "Anyone who doesn't have a temper is not worth a dime." That became a point of confusion in me from that day on. I wanted terribly to please the "big people" in my life. My other motivation to conformity was to escape being disciplined or punished. Now a conflicting message had begun from the big people that said I shouldn't adapt. This double message was pushed further and further down inside as I continued my attempts to please everyone. My performance level increased each year.

Even in adolescence, there was little conscious rebellion. In retrospect, I know there was a major war going on inside of me. But I had been taught well. Good girls did what was expected of them. Everything that was good or right in life came from parents and authority figures. It was neither ladylike nor Christian to display my feelings. It was all quite easy because it was such a neatly wrapped package. Rigidity had relieved me of responsibility, excused me from the necessity to think, eliminated my having to make decisions and erased any trend toward creativity.

I accepted on a conscious level the script that was handed to me almost without question. You know, as I look back on the person I was, I hardly recognize me. I know one thing for certain—I repressed any need to know or be myself.

Philosophers have contemplated three particular questions throughout the centuries:

1. Who am I?
2. Where did I come from?
3. Where am I going?

The second two questions may arouse curiosity and cause enough concern for a search for security. However, if I am not decisive on question one, "Who am I?", I'll experience fear, contempt, and ultimately apathy. Confusion about your own person is like a poison to your system. I know—I went through all three phases: fear, contempt and then apathy.

What stops you from opening up to your feelings and talking to yourself? The same problem I had, and the same problem everyone else has—*fear*!

Fear is the first basic feeling we have. We spend a great portion of our lives defending ourselves against our fears.

You fear looking into the mirror. You fear the guilt of a dishonest past. You fear becoming vulnerable to another person or the challenge of honesty. You fear rejection. You fear having to face your real self and philosophies and feelings that might replace the role you have been playing. Most of all you fear you!

So what can be done about it?

1. The willingness to begin taking that first step is so important. Small efforts are not to be scoffed at by any of us. The willingness to try—to begin—to make an effort is a necessity.

2. Begin your self-evaluation in love. Don't set out to criticize and condemn yourself. Judgment is not your aim. Self-realization and understanding is the desired result.

3. Respect yourself and your own right to be a person.

4. Learn to realize what your fears are and how to encounter them.

5. Listen to others react to you without provoking your defenses.

6. Learn to trust your unconscious and your own feelings.

7. Learn to accept *your* feelings as being *really you*.

8. Deal with whatever God has to say to you and then interpret your feelings.

A great deal has been written on this subject so let me capsulize it in a few words. All of us have four sides to ourselves:

1. *The Actual Self*—This is our real self, the self that is our total being. It includes our conscious and our unconscious. We often overlook that. Our unconscious

logs up every experience and event throughout our life, then files and stores it. It is with us twenty-four hours a day. You seldom get to know who this total being is. Why? There are many reasons—time, fear, permission, tradition, knowledge, and circumstances.

2. *The Idealized Self*—This is that person you always wanted to be. You had those daydreams and fantasies of being a singer, a famous politician or a Billy Graham. Sure you did. I've always dreamed of being neat and orderly. I can look at another woman and tell if she has a nicely kept purse with everything in perfect order. And I can fantasize myself as a singer. I can actually hear the notes, feel my breathing and taste the thrill of applause.

3. *The Role Self*—This is the self that you are playing now. We all play a certain amount of roles. In one day, you may go from being the head of a household to an employer at work or to a professor of an evening school class. All are distinct roles, but actually this is not the role self I am speaking of at this point. What I'm referring to is when we put on a role that is the complete opposite of our real self. We force ourself into a straight jacket that squeezes the life out of us. Call it being phony, being a hypocrite, living a lie, over adapting or "keeping up with the Joneses"—but whatever you call it matters little—it's painful, terribly painful!

4. *The Self Everyone Sees*—People see a mixture of all of these. No one can fool all of the people all of the time. No, not even if we have ourselves fooled.

Occasionally, when we feel we are presenting

ourselves as towers of strength to the public, a friend will surprise us with the question, ''Are you all right? You certainly have appeared upset lately!''

Even the roles we play take on such a variety of faces that people see us differently than we suspect. Our environment will cause us to behave in a way that surprises some. We make a statement or react in a manner out of character to us. This frightens us and confuses others as they formulate opinions of us. Although it may appear ''out of character'' it is still me—my feelings, part of my unconscious and I must accept that.

Your goal should now be to work toward melting 1, 2, and 4 together. Here's how it's done. Get to know your actual self—the real you. Be alone with yourself. Write down your likes and dislikes, your prejudices and your fears. Reflect upon your past and your parents. What has influenced you the most? How are you like your parents? What characteristics have you gotten from them? Do you feel good about yourself? Are there changes you need to make?

If you are uncomfortable with yourself or you feel bad about yourself, then it would be good to seek the help of a counselor or therapist. A professional can help you be objective with yourself as well as support you emotionally through the needed changes.

The work you do on yourself will bring positive changes. The good feeling and experiences that emerge from these positive changes will serve as an impetus to more changes until you are in a good place. You are aware of your being, your feelings, and your needs.

Slowly your actual self and your ideal self are united within a realistic setting. Do you hear what I am suggesting? As your goals and dreams become a part of you, you can achieve them with your new awareness and confidence.

Note the word "realistic." Our idealized self, our goals, or dreams should be kept in the realm of reality. Otherwise we create unnecessary conflicts and pressures.

Now what happens to the role self and the self people see? When you are satisfied and content with you, there will be no need for play acting any more. You can throw away the scripts. You'll play yourself now. Your family and friends will see the real you—the best you—and they'll love and respect you. Not all of them will, but the ones who really love you will accept you. No, I can't give you a "happy ever after" promise. Unfortunately, some people want to trap others, hold them back or force them into a distasteful mold. These people, however, will never be satisfied with you, so why continue the show for their sake?

Let me outline for you some simple suggestions that will help you get better acquainted with yourself.

1. Give yourself some time to be alone with yourself. It will never happen unless you make it happen. When you are alone, spend some time writing down anything that comes to your mind. Question yourself concerning your feelings.

2. Keep a daily diary on your feelings. At the end of the day record your highs and lows as well as the events that triggered these feelings.

3. Compare yourself with your parents. Write down all the similarities in attitudes and behavior between you and your parents.

4. List your goals and priorities. What motives are behind your present goals?

5. Set new goals. If you have been rather passive toward yourself, set some goals for yourself now.

6. Begin a reading program. There are some excellent books available that are written specifically to help you get in touch with yourself. Sound information will always help you.

7. Mental stimulation is important. Start forcing yourself to think in all areas of yourself. Give yourself permission to think, to make decisions, to be knowledgeable.

8. Become aware of your own body. Begin a program of physical fitness.

9. Become aware of your appearance. If you don't like what you see and what you feel, do something about it.

10. Join a group led by a confident professional.

11. Search out your spiritual side. Do you have any relationship with God? What is it, and how does it affect you?

12. Begin to build self-respect. See yourself from positive eyes.

13. Make friends with alert, caring people who can positively affect you.

14. Start simple and work up. Allow yourself small victories rather than waiting for the big ones.
15. Learn how to get positive recognition and love when you need it.

Let's Get Motivated

I believe, as in any other goal you wish to accomplish, that you must first make up your mind to do so. You must want this for yourself — bad enough to do whatever it takes to achieve it for you. Several times a week people come to my office seeking help, advice and information on problem solving. Many times when nothing positive happens, I question their "want to." This is usually followed by a questioning look from the client. The point I have to make to the person in need is that all the help in the world will not change negative behavior if he or she does not want to do so. I mean by this, *really* want to do so.

The first step in any type of growth is a mental and emotional commitment to the task. This will be easier when you are properly motivated. I know what you are probably thinking right now. How many, many people have said these words, "But, I'm really not motivated." Or, others say, "I just don't care—it doesn't matter anymore." You will accomplish nothing of worth in life if you're not motivated.

Here you are. You have come to the conclusion that you have little self-awareness. You are reading a script.

You have adopted a life-style that was handed to you. This negative part of your life has caused you many heartaches and cost you a number of friends. Still, you don't seem motivated enough to begin a program of action.

The issues involved have got to be great enough to force your will to make a decision. You've got to be convinced in your mind. I personally believe that *facts* are impressive tools of changing behavior.

Perhaps the following suggestions can develop a program of motivation in you.

1. Take a long look at yourself. Decide where you've been, where you are now and where you want to go.
2. Fantasize what you would like to be like, where you would like to be and what you would like to be doing in six months.
3. Set some realistic long range and short range goals. Write them down in order of importance.
4. Question yourself as to how you affect those closest to you. Does your attitude motivate them or discourage them?
5. What five changes could you make in your personality to effect a better relationship with your family and friends?
6. How do you feel about your own body? Are there changes that should be made?
7. Have you been the cause of unfortunate situations in your home or business? How could these be corrected?

8. How important is your family to you? Important enough to work toward changes?
9. How important is your employment?
10. How important is your life to you? Are you making it count?

Decision Time

Now it's time to make a decision about you. You have considered the problems and the risks involved in not working on new attitudes and behavior. Now the ball is in your hands to decide on action or not.

The important part of this decision is your realizing you have the ability or the capacity to change—and more specifically to communicate. This is not to say it would be easy, or that a lot of work is not involved. I am saying that the hope is in your willingness to act and to do something with yourself.

To refer back to what has already been said, the need must be significant enough to make you want to change.

Let me illustrate with a very common occurance. A couple comes to me on the verge of divorce. The anger is near the explosion level, feelings are tense and I quickly evaluate the situation to be a crisis state. Of course, through the years there have been multitudes of hurts and disappointments. They have not communicated verbally and emotionally and have grown further and further apart. Now, of late the wife has announced, "If we don't correct our problems, I'm leaving." When the husband becomes convinced that her words are not mere threats, he concedes and agrees to come in for counseling. When I inquired as to why they waited until it was almost too late, he replied, "I didn't know anything was wrong." I'm quite sure the husband had an idea that his marriage was not what it should have been, but only when he was faced with the reality of divorce, did his need prompt him into doing something about his problem. For every case like this one, I have hundreds more.

It always amazes me—and yes, somewhat angers me when I'm awakened in the middle of the night by a "concerned," "anxious parent." Perhaps I should describe the circumstances a little more. The part about waking me up is not the rub. Certainly I'm not normally angered over a concerned parent. I have worked closely with young people for many years. My love for teenagers stems from examples set before me in my adolescent years. I love their enthusiasm and feel very strongly the pressures they experience during these crucial years. I've led out in organizations that deal with kids on spiritual and moral issues. I feel strongly the need to provide camp programs, athletic programs and youth Bible studies in the community. I have always backed churches that would provide sound, enthusiastic youth programs. But during these years, I've encountered a shocking number of parents who radically opposed any spiritual involvement for their children. Often a teenager would plead with me to talk to the parents and attempt to explain what being a Christian really meant. I would grant the youngster's request and call on the parents. Sometimes, I would approach them from every side, but to no avail. The answer was a flat, "No!" They were definite on the opinion that their child needed no spiritual influences.

I'm not suggesting that the parents did not love and care for their child. They were caring people and wanted the best for the family. However, they were denying their child of spiritual feelings and a beautiful part of life. The Scripture states that the evidence of the Spirit is love, joy, peace, longsuffering, gentleness, and goodness. The denial of these positive experiences is an opening to negative ones for the child.

Who calls me in the middle of the night? Who screams the loudest? Who demands immediate attention and action? Who questions, "Why?" You've guessed it by now—the very ones who sent me away with the comment, "No religion for our kid."

They re-evaluate their position, however, and take long looks at their own condition when a crisis occurs.

I don't know about you, but I was just as bad. I've already explained to you in this chapter how naive I was to my own feelings. I've tried to explain as honestly as I know how my dullness to my own reality. I hate to admit it, but had several crises not come into my life, I would probably still be in this not so good position. I would be living up to only half of my potential. I certainly wouldn't be in the counseling field. I might have gone through life apathetic to it all and never known what I had missed.

Developing Your Sensitivity

Awareness is the essence of communication. This awareness begins with self—your own honest, vital oneness with you will ignite a sensitivity toward others.

Let's define perception and sensitivity. The dictionary defines them as the following. To Perceive: (1) To be aware of through senses; (2) To take in with the mind; (3) To understand, comprehend. Sense: (1) The power of the mind to know what happens outside itself; (2) A feeling, a sense of warmth; (3) A faculty, perception, or a sensation not based on the five senses: a sixth sense; (4) Sense applies to the power of the mind to respond to stimulation from within or without and accord it proper recognition: "He has a sense of well-being." Sensitivity: The quality or state of being sensitive: sentimentality and sensitivity, not in the maudlin but in the highest sense, are perhaps the greatest and most important qualities in a good mother.

Learn to See and Hear and Feel

Surprisingly enough, the majority of people wander through life unaware of people, places, or things. Life has little meaning. Events in daily life have only slight significance. These people plod through their humdrum existence by habitual behavior. This life drama could be described as "meaningless" or "going nowhere." The people they meet will consider them dull and unattractive.

Should this description fit you, I would strongly suggest that you begin a definite program for yourself in developing awareness and sensitivity.

I will first list some characteristics of the person who has not developed his sensitivity in order that you can more clearly recognize yourself.

1. Finds it difficult to remember events of the past.
2. Seems to forget orders and instructions easily.
3. Forgets people, names, faces, events.
4. Appears dull to those around him.
5. Procrastinates.
6. Lacks in motivation.
7. Says the wrong thing at the wrong time.
8. Often misses "the point" in a conversation.
9. Appears "slow" in the thinking processes.
10. Is often accused of hurting someone by inappropriate words.
11. Finds it difficult to "make good things happen" for himself and others.

12. Life's activities are conducted by mere habit leaving a boring existence to the person involved.

13. Little or no goals for the present or future.

14. Finds it almost impossible to put himself in the place of another. Cannot empathize.

15. Not in contact with any feelings.

16. Is not involved in any of the arts such as: music, art, dance, sculpturing, etc.

17. Finds little appreciation for nature.

18. Is not aroused by touch.

19. Avoids people touching him or getting too close.

20. Is not aware of his body.

Sensitivity grows out of self-awareness. When you get in touch with your own feelings, your ability to "tune in" to another person's feelings is far greater. As you allow yourself to experience your feelings, your senses come alive. Life takes on new meaning and you become involved with sensations that add flavor to living. Some of these sensations will be frightening in that they are new. You'll be uncomfortable at times with their intensity, still, the pleasure far outweighs the discomfort.

Learn To Listen

No element of communication is more important than the art of listening. Learning to listen and to really hear swings open the door to effective communication.

I want to begin with the most simplistic form of listening—*appearing* to listen. It was distressing to me (and still is) during my silent years to observe how people listened but didn't hear. It was horrifying, however, to realize that many did not even go through the pretense of listening. I have had it reported to me in counseling sessions in the following ways:

> "I've asked him direct questions at the breakfast table, and he continued reading the paper."
>
> "My wife and I have gone for weeks without speaking—oh, maybe a ritualistic 'good morning' or 'have a good day.' "
>
> "I walk into the room, try to open a conversation, and my father continues to be entranced with his television."
>
> "The only time I ever get a sentence out of my mother is when she's angry."
>
> "I can't remember my parents asking me about my interests and needs."
>
> "How can we talk? We never see each other."
>
> "I've literally grabbed the book out of his hand, and still he refused to comment."
>
> "When I try to talk to her or discuss our problems, she walks out of the house."
>
> "At meal times, I'm totally discounted. It's as though I weren't there."
>
> "My husband won't talk. His only comment is, 'I haven't anything worth saying.' "

These quotes illustrate the giant of all discounts. When we refuse to speak, or to recognize the other or to be available, we are actually saying, ''I wish you weren't here!'' This strikes at the very core of the other's self-esteem, bringing them pain and feelings of rejection. When this continues, you can be confident that bizarre behavior will emerge.

Sometimes a heavy schedule, problems, physical pain and circumstances will cause us to be non-communicating. We don't mean to ignore, but we do. Regardless of the purity of our motives, the hurt is the same and the damage severe.

If you catch yourself feeling ''bogged down'' and you sense you have not been fair in your availability, say so! This will be a beautiful occasion to express your needs and share your burdens with those closest to you.

The second step is to be quiet enough to hear. The number one barricade to hearing is you! Sometimes the simple decision to talk less will mean an automatic listen more. I'm not implying that you should immediately take a vow to silence. This would really stir up some commotion at home or work. I'm not suggesting extremes.

For example, when you're eating a meal at home, and the youngsters are all wanting to talk—let them! Some nights, give them the floor. Your interest will spur them on, and you'll be delighted when the sharing is over.

Another suggestion to facilitate listening is to set aside a definite time per day or week for a family conference. So often we have to force ourselves to do what is necessary. A definite time eliminates a lot of unpleasant conversations at meal times or at inappropriate moments.

Setting aside time to listen and giving the other person permission to speak through your attention is only the beginning!

The next move is to develop an interest in other people. You move outside of your own self, and you become attentive to the needs of others. This is the caring part of communication. To state it very simply, you *want* to hear what others are saying. You are no longer going through the ritual of what appears to be listening. You are working at understanding the total message coming from the other person. Yes, I would call it work.

When a person comes to me for counseling, I'm often exhausted when the hour concludes. I work hard at hearing what my client is saying. The words that are spoken are not always the true message that is being transmitted.

In order to listen properly and be involved in your messages, I will have to put aside for the moment some of my thoughts. Haven't you experienced many times conversing with someone who continually breaks in on your sentences? Your thoughts are springboards to what he wants to say. You are acutely aware that your conversation merely gives him time to think about his next comments. What do you end up doing? You end the conversation, walk away, bow out gracefully or determine never to try it again with this person.

Listen for the psychological messages being spoken to

you. Not too many people in our society are able to be open, honest, uninhibited in all their remarks. The needs, pains, or words of friendship may all be wrapped in social conversation that is neat, polite, and meaningless. The accomplished listener will hear and pull out those messages that are hidden and address himself to those.

Several years ago a lovely woman in the community tragically took her life. Her death took everyone by surprise. For weeks after the sad event, I heard continual remarks such as: "I had no idea anything was even bothering her . . ." "She never said anything to any of us about her problems." "I thought she was very happy and content with life." Now, I'm aware that some people mask their feelings well; still, I couldn't help but wonder if she had tried to express her pain. Was anyone listening for the real messages? Obviously not or perhaps all would have been different.

See What's Around You

Communication is enhanced when you begin using your eyes. Look at the person to whom you are speaking. What are his eyes saying? Is there obvious fear in this person? Do you see concern or heartache on his face? Does his forehead tell you he's tired? His head, back and shoulders will clue you immediately as to his condition.

Likewise you give away a lot of secrets through your eyes. Your eyes can express what words cannot.

I've sat through many social conversations and

noticed the participants were not looking at one another. In fact, there seemed to be a definite effort to avoid eye contact. As the evening went on, boundaries were clearly established and everyone stayed in his or her designated zone.

How Do You Feel?

The sense of touch is needed and should be developed as much as hearing and seeing. When this subject is considered, there are usually many barriers surrounding it. As infants and children we were sensitive and sensuous, loving to touch and be touched. Time and circumstances changed all of that, and we learned from the world around us to throw up boundaries. The boundaries appear to be a necessity for survival against the hurts of life.

Evaluate your own sense of touch and what you do with it. What has been your pattern of touch this past year? Do you enjoy touching others or do you avoid all physical contact? Do you feel yourself withdrawing when someone reaches out to you?

When I was doing my practice teaching for my credential, I had a blind boy in my class. He made a profound impression on me and I shall always be thankful for the lessons he taught me. This young man was completely blind and had been so since birth. He was a brilliant boy and studied independently as though he had no handicap. Almost immediately, I realized his exceptional sense of touch. I wore a gold charm bracelet to school and he could identify even the smallest charm. The communication between us grew not so much out of his sensitive touch but rather in his willingness to touch. Naturally, his inability to see motivated his willingness to touch. Nevertheless, we learned to say so much by sharing in this way.

On many occasions I asked myself, "Why had I neglected this particular sense in the past?" I realized quickly the losses I had experienced from not touching.

Developing Your Senses Through Nature

It might be easier for you to begin developing your senses through the world around you. If you are not a sensitive person and you lack in this area, you've missed out on a great deal of beauty and ecstasy. A sunset, a warm, gentle breeze, the scent of jasmine have all passed you by. Life's details of elegance have melted together into an unsavory mixture.

Make a decision today to start seeing, hearing and feeling the world around you. You have a lot of living to do, so you might as well experience it all. There are multitudes of delicious feelings that you deserve. Why else would God provide them for you?

If I were to live to be 150 years old I could never forget the beauty of the Hawaiian sunset. My daughter and I spent several weeks in Hawaii a few years ago. Nature seemed to reach out and grab our hearts and minds on every side. We felt almost bizarre as our senses experienced the fragrance of the flowers, the ocean spray and the clear skies. But I shall never forget our last night in Maui. We wanted to take pictures of the sunset. We waited on the quiet sand for the time to come. Then, as though God wanted to give His own special gift to Karen and me, we experienced a sunset that to this day remains indescribable. The ecstasy of the moment was a spiritual time for both of us. The awareness of our own feelings brought other feelings. Happy tears came from the occasion as well as sad tears over having to leave such a cradle of God's handiwork.

Perhaps you can't go to Hawaii, but here are some suggestions that will be equally satisfactory in developing your senses:

1. When you wake up in the morning, look outside for something you have never seen before.

2. Listen for the first sounds you hear.

3. On your way to work, take alternate routes and notice new sights.

4. Look for small parts of nature that you may have missed such as a baby bird, or a rosebud.

5. Work at listening to sounds—all sounds—loud and soft. Try to identify them all and see their significance.

6. Take off your shoes and walk in the grass or through a puddle. If it's been raining, sink your toes into some mud. What does this experience remind you of in your past?

7. Walk in the warm rain.

8. Lie in the sun and let its warm rays say something to you.

9. Touch things you haven't touched in years such as:

the velvety petals of a rose, the whiskers on your father's face, or the back of a baby's little head and neck.

10. Look into the faces of people. All people, young and old have something to say to you.

Now you are ready to become sensitive to those around you. Communication begins with sensitivity. As you are unable to sense the needs and feelings of others, you become more capable of communicating properly.

The word perception enters into this idea. How do you perceive yourself, the world around you, the people you meet, your family and your friends? Do you see them as human beings needing love and understanding? When you enter a room, are you able to sense the happiness, anger, joy or conflict that might exist in the minds of those present? Or are you so far removed from those closest to you that you trod under foot their feelings with your words?

Are you too busy to be aware of the loneliness, fears, and anxieties that exist within the hearts and minds of loved ones? Do you perceive your associates as robots who are to respond to your commands and wishes? Do you look at the world as threatening and evil? Do you expect the people in your world to be liars, cheaters and thieves? If your answers to these questions are in the affirmative, then you will communicate by your attitude to those around you that it is you that is against the world.

On the other hand, if you look at people as basically good and you have faith in them, this hope and expectancy will be communicated to them. Isn't this the beginning of sensitivity in communication?

When a person comes to me for counseling, I look at him from eyes of love and hope. I expect him to get well and to work out his problems. I have learned that I can accept this person, regardless of his problem or background, and I can love him and expect him to be okay.

Sensitivity and perception takes practice. It also takes effort! It might even feel foreign to you when you first begin. You may have been so busy that you have lost all sensitivity. I know a man who has a great deal of love for people. In fact, I would stake my life on the fact he wouldn't or couldn't physically hurt anyone. He would never hurt anyone emotionally. Still, he does, and his behavior has caused him loneliness and pain. His problem is not an unattractive appearance or an inhibited personality. He has no problem verbalizing his thoughts and opinions. To be honest, his intelligence and humor bring him a lot of praise. In intimate relationships, however, he's experiencing failure because he lacks sensitivity. He does not have the ability to relate to the needs of other people. He is not able to feel what others are feeling until it is too late.

I remember the inadequacy I felt when I lost the use of my voice. "How could I possibly relate to others?" was the question that haunted me. A few casual statements made by friends and co-workers still remain with me. I want to share them with you because they gave me hope and made me aware that sensitivity was a form of communication.

As I mentioned to you earlier, I first lost my voice while teaching school. I taught out the year with a small, weak voice. One day at lunch another teacher sat down next to me. He confessed to me, "You'll never know how pleasant it is to be around someone with such a gentle voice. You seem to calm us all down." I had never thought of my voice as gentle. What was a liability to me had been experienced as an asset by another.

Another morning when I was walking out to meet my class on the playground, I waved at a couple of the mothers who were playground helpers. They ran over to me thinking I had said something to them which they had not heard. One of them said to me, "We never hear what you say, but we always know you're glad to see us by the smile on your face." Perhaps if I had been able to yell out a greeting, I would not have smiled. It was actually the warmth of a smile that was most appreciated.

I remember the time when touch became more meaningful during a counseling session. A woman had been terribly distressed. She was extremely angry and not willing to do much about her problem. Although she had made a giant step and come in for counseling, she was withdrawn and reluctant to share with me. Only few words were spoken. We sat quietly for a long period of time. She appeared to become more and more tense. Finally, I reached over and held her hands. I said nothing, but kept gently stroking her hands. Within seconds, the tears began to flow. The barriers came tumbling down. We were ready to work.

Here are some simple tips and practical exercises to help you become more sensitive:

1. Become visually aware of the world around you.
2. Develop a sense of touch.
3. Close your eyes and fantasize lovely scenes.
4. Try to guess what the other members of your family are thinking when you're not quite sure.
5. Inquire (at the right moments) as to what makes others very happy or extremely sad.
6. Spend more time at the dinner table being quiet and listening to what others have to say.
7. Try to get alone with each member of the family and inquire if there is anything they need.
8. Set aside times during the week to spend alone with each member of the family so they will feel free to talk to you.
9. Don't look angry or shocked when people confide in you.
10. *Think* before you speak.
11. Think about the feelings of others before you give orders to them.
12. Learn more about the way your spouse and children think and feel by reading books, watching them, talking to them and playing with them.
13. Think of your family as friends.
14. Learn to be alone with nature and appreciate its beauty.

15. Learn to be alone with yourself and enjoy it. If you are sensitive to your feelings, you will be more sensitive to others.

16. Cry with people when they cry. Try to *feel* their hurt.

17. Get excited with people when good things happen to them. Don't pour cold water on their good times.

18. Accept other people's problems as seriously as you do your own.

19. Care about the other person's comfort as much as your own.

20. Do something "special" to or for those closest to you.

Social Communication

No friends since can't remember when,
But a friend I haven't been.
So wrapped up in me today,
I share no joy along the way.

You've been feeling lonely and empty a lot lately. It's finally hit you that you have very few friends. Sure, you have some acquaintances at work, but when you go home you're alone. You make an occasional attempt to go out and meet others, but it never seems to work out. Weeks pass by and you receive no recognition, no love and no support. There's also no fun in your life. Most of your pleasure is derived from work. When the chance to socialize comes to you, you quickly find reasons why you can't take advantage of it. A part of you wants very much to meet new people and make new friends. Another part of you is almost relieved when circumstances prohibit you from groups and parties.

You may be screaming to yourself right now, "That's me! That's me!" There could be many deep problems that have contributed to making you this way. I'm not going to attempt to name them. What I am going to do is discuss your social communication and suggest ways you can improve on it.

I'll be honest with you—the majority of people who visited my office last year fit that description fully. Their plea was simply, "Please help me make friends and keep relationships." Usually, by the time someone comes to me with such a need, they have already experienced many failures. There's been enough hurt to cause them to reach out and say to me, "I can't go on like this anymore."

People do need people, and when you and I realize that fact we're on our way. When the reality and the immensity of this finally hits us, the impact can cause us quite a jolt. There are various reactions when it occurs. For example:

> Some will become angry at the world for being so rotten.
>
> Some will have regrets for all the lost years.
>
> Some will continue to deny the facts.
>
> Some will blame it all on everyone else.
>
> Some will indulge in self-pity.
>
> Some will look for sympathy.
>
> Some will withdraw further.

Some will attack the only close friends or family available.

Some will become more obnoxious in social communication.

Some will recognize the problem and ask for help.

Obviously, the first nine reactions won't work. In fact, if a person responds in any of the ways mentioned except the last one, he experiences a setback. These are rationalizations and defenses that fight bitterly against your progress.

Some of you may be puzzled as to whether or not you have a significant problem in communicating socially. "Maybe everyone else is out of step and not me." "Perhaps I'm not meant to have close friends." "Who needs them? Who needs anyone—I have myself." If you've made these statements or similar ones, you're aware of a need, but you can't quite face it as yet.

The following questions may help you focus in on your need. Answer them honestly.

1. Do you have any close friends?
2. Do you have anyone who will confide in you?
3. Do you have anyone to whom you can go in times of trouble? Will this person accept you regardless of your problem?
4. Do you have good rapport with the people at work?
5. Are you often in the center of conflict at work?
6. Does your family talk to you freely?

7. Do most of your family discussions end up in arguments?

8. Is your family uneasy or frightened of you?

9. Do you often get asked out to social functions?

10. When you entertain guests, do they often return the favor?

11. Do social acquaintances feel free and comfortable around you? (You can usually tell!)

12. Do you feel at ease around social acquaintances?

13. Do you feel at ease in a new social situation?

14. Do most of your social conversations end up as a soap box for your favorite cause?

15. When you leave a social occasion, do you often have the feeling you talked too much?

16. Do you feel "left out" at social gatherings?

17. Do you behave as though you are better than anyone else—or not as good as anyone else?

18. Are you afraid of meeting and talking to the opposite sex?

19. Are you threatened by members of your own sex?

20. Do you usually end up losing good relationships?

These questions will apply to both single and married people. I realize that these two categories have problems unique to their situations; however, principles of social communication are the same for both singles and marrieds!

How do you feel about your answers? If you were

honest in your answers, you are more aware now of your ability in communicating socially.

How To Improve Your Social Communication

Eliminate The Fear. If I'm not afraid of you when you talk to me, you will have taken a giant step toward building a relationship. "Ease"—that's an important word to you right now. You want to put the person or persons with whom you are communicating at ease!

In the second chapter, we discussed the subject of fear and how it throws up barriers to communication. No one is completely exempt from fears. We all run the same risks when we consider relationships. Because of the common element of fear in all of us, you need to begin your communication by eliminating it both within yourself and in the other person.

Regardless of the situation (home, work, dinner party, church, club meeting), you will want to take the initial step to put the other or others at ease. "It's not all that easy," you're thinking right now. Let's look at some obvious ways you can put people at ease:

1. Decide before the event begins that *you're* going to be comfortable.

2. Do whatever you need to do to feel good about *yourself.*

3. Decide on taking the *initiative* in communication.

4. When you are introduced, look directly at the person.

5. Focus all your attention and energy on him; not on yourself, not on what he's thinking about you, not on clever things to say!

6. At the initial introduction, do not try to be a "personality plus" person. The other person is the important one.

7. Smile in a poised, genuine manner. The smile must reflect your desire to know this person—not a "happy image."

8. Say the person's name after it is given to you.

9. Reach out your hand to him. If the other person reacts positively to your gesture, shake his hand. When you grasp his hand, tell him everything is okay!

10. Continue to focus your interest and energy on the other person as the conversation continues.

Be Conscious Of The Other Person More Than Yourself. Over a year ago, a handsome young man sat in my office and shared with me that he had no friends. This was hard for me to believe. His basic complaint was that he didn't talk to people because he didn't know how. He said:

> "*I* go to a party, but *I* don't talk to anyone. *I'm* always afraid they won't like *me*. *I've* really always been a little quiet. *I* don't feel like *I* have an exciting personality. *I'm* afraid *I* won't have anything to say. *I* guess *I'm* also afraid they'll talk about something *I* know nothing about."

What do you hear in his statements? Immediately you experience his fear, don't you? He was quite open and willing to work on his overall fear. We tracked down some of it's origin in the weeks to come. I do believe, however, that he experienced a great breakthrough when he finally realized that everyone else has similar fears.

The next move was to make him aware of all the "I's" and "me's" in the statement of his problem.

He thought he had to perform. The spotlight was on *him*. Would he say it right? Would his personality be exciting? Does he know enough to hold a conversation? I don't doubt he would retreat from conversation. That's quite a trip to lay on himself.

Communication is not entertainment! Communication is sharing. Realize this, and the burden becomes lighter. The whole idea of communicating will be less threatening. This was what I told the gentleman along with the following advice:

It is not so important for someone to like you immediately. Don't worry about this. Concentrate on conveying to the person that you like him. People are drawn more quickly to genuine, caring people than to the "personality boys." Be interested in the other person. Respond to what he says rather than trying to drum up interesting material. If a subject comes up that is unfamiliar to you—all the better! This will give you a marvelous chance to say to him, "I need you." This will give him an opportunity to share with you what is of great interest to him. While he talks, you can relax a bit and experience more of this person. Your patient listening will trigger the same positive reactions in him when you begin to share.

My client contracted with me to try this at least once a week for six months. It worked for him as it has for so many. He learned the simple truth that people respond to people who respond to them.

Be Aware Of The Common Denominators In All Of Us. You want to be an individual. Of course you do—so do I. Regardless of our unique qualities, we must all concede to certain basic similarities. We all have the same basic emotional needs. Somehow, someway we learn to swallow the notion that we are the only ones with needs.

> We all need love.
> We all need security.
> We all need recognition.
> We all need expression.
> We all need peak experiences.

When you are with someone, you may tend to disregard his needs. You do this by allowing yourself to believe he is all-sufficient. I know—I've met them also. Some people always appear so in control, so together. How could they possibly need or want anything I have to say or give?

Don't let looks fool you. Oftentimes, the ones who appear the strongest are actually the most needy. Their behavior is merely a cover-up of many hurts and needs.

How does this help you in your communication problems? It's simple. See yourself as providing a service. You're not actually asking the other person for anything—not for recognition, not for approval, not for an instant relationship. Rather, you are there to meet some of his needs. See every person as having needs. Some may fool you. Others may express it more openly. It doesn't matter—you must believe that most people with whom you communicate need something that you have to give. Anyone would appreciate your attention. Often, when you meet someone, you can fill a lonely spot. Many simply need someone with whom they can talk. When you meet the needs of other people, they will like you. They will enjoy you and enjoy your communication with them. You see, we're all quite selfish. We enjoy people who meet our needs.

Provide a Non-Threatening Climate. Are you one of those people who make great first impressions, but the fireworks come later? You can walk into a new group and make instant friends. But, what happens to them all? Here you are—the life of the party but the loneliest guy in town.

This situation throws all of us at one time or another. I'm always amazed at the people who claim loneliness to me. Often, they are celebrities in their field and appear to be surrounded by people.

If you are in this situation, something is running your friends away. Why try to fool ourselves. Something you are doing is running your friends away.

Let's take a realistic look at the problem. If you make good first impressions, you must have plenty going for you. Providing you don't have a serious problem in your personality, something happens when you start getting close to people. Check the climate you provide for people. Is it threatening? How do people feel around you?

I knew a couple back East who were delightful on first impression. After attending several small dinner parties with them, I became aware that their presence produced uncomfortable feelings in me. It wasn't long until I sensed the same discomfort in others. Here's what happened continuously throughout the evening:

1. He dominated the conversation.
2. He questioned (either verbally or by his voice tone) every statement made by others.
3. He corrected statements made by others, or added more information to them.
4. He provoked controversial issues.
5. He always pushed his "pet philosophy."
6. He used his position as power to persuade and dominate the group.
7. He left little time for anyone else to speak.
8. He raised his voice to gain more attention.
9. He embarrassed at least one individual directly.
10. He used a great deal of sarcasm.

The husband's attitude produced a threatening climate.

No one could relax. In fact, we were all exhausted from defending ourselves or escaping an embarrassing situation.

His wife was sensitive to what was happening. She tried desperately to rescue him, ward off arguments, and change controversial subjects. Nothing worked. In fact, her noble attempts contributed to the tragedy. Her frustration made all of us even more intensely uneasy.

What happened with our new friendship? What do you think happened? I dropped out and so did everyone else. There's not a very happy ending to this story. Unfortunately, there never is for the ones who fail to provide an understanding and supportive environment.

Respect And Courtesy Go A Long Way. This is really getting down to the basic stuff, isn't it? Respect— courtesy—they seem so simple and so basic! Why even waste a page on such a subject?

Time and time again people come to me expecting the magic answers. Their problem is keeping friends past the initial introduction. They are confident that there is a deep hidden mystery surrounding their situation. It doesn't take long for me to realize that the mystery is no more than common, ordinary good manners. This answer is usually distasteful to the individual for several reasons:

1. It's certainly not dramatic in the least.

2. The simplicity of the whole idea is rather embarrassing.

3. The cure can be effected quite rapidly.

4. The "ball" is in their hands to act upon a change.

I have to bring in my own feelings here. This is a matter that definitely bothers me. During my silent years, I was sickened by the lack of courtesy in social communication. After observing many upsetting scenes, I came to my own conclusions as to the source of such a problem. The rudeness displayed was traced back to: 1) A lack of respect for oneself, 2) A lack of respect for the other or others, 3) A lack of training as a child in simple good manners, 4) An "I don't care" attitude for life in general.

Regardless of the origin, the problem is there and most of us are usually not willing to stick around until a solution is found. If this is your problem, here are some important steps to take:

1. Look at me when I'm talking.

2. Give me your attention when we're trying to communicate (don't walk away).

3. Attempt to hear what I'm saying before making negative judgments.

4. Assume what I'm saying is true.

5. Assume what I'm saying can be validated.

6. Assume I have some knowledge or background in the matter.

7. Assume I am deserving of your respect (regardless of race, money, education, position).

8. Avoid interrupting me when I'm speaking.

9. Avoid raising your voice in order to make a stronger point.

10. Avoid challenging every issue or fact.

11. Avoid criticizing or name calling.

12. Avoid attacking my character or person when your argument gets weak.

13. Avoid using your position as a power over me.

14. Be aware of your body language and the negative message it can convey.

15. Mellow out your speech. A caustic tongue can do a great deal of damage.

I recall attending several social engagements with the same group of people. Perhaps if I share with you what happened, it will reinforce my point. On each occasion, I experienced myself as "not okay" within about thirty minutes after the group gathered. There was a gentleman present whom I am certain felt called by God to keep all of us straight. To sum it up, he knew all, had been everywhere and had done everything. There was no need for any of us to share our thoughts. As least, that's the way he made us feel. An expert was in our midst who wanted to teach us—not share with us.

It was interesting to note the reactions of the various individuals involved. One or two stayed away from him. The hostess attempted to rescue the situation. One man always aligned himself with him in an attempt to be on the winning side. One couple left early as a reaction to his insults. Several found him amusing and nervously laughed and joked during the discussions. One man confronted him and argued intensely throughout the evening. And he had two who sat at his feet as followers learning from the master-teacher.

Avoid Offensive Behavior Or Appearance. This section is as basic as the last section on respect and courtesy. It remains on top of the list if you want to keep friends. I'm convinced that it's the obvious "little things" that drive people away.

Of course, you don't deliberately offend people. This is exactly why an occasional evaluation of yourself is helpful. Take a long look at you. Ask your best friend for advice.

A check list is included here to help you evaluate yourself. The information comes from hundreds of interviews I have made in the past few years. The purpose of the interviews was to determine the habits or characteristics that make us want to avoid a person. They are as follows (not in any particular order of importance):

1. Dirty or unkept appearance
2. Unpleasant odors
3. Hair that is not combed or is dirty
4. Wrinkled clothes
5. Obesity
6. Gum chewing
7. Cracking ice

8. Smoking
9. Obvious nervous moves or gestures
10. Loudness
11. Crudeness
12. Indiscreet conversation
13. Demanding and critical attitude
14. Negative attitude and conversation
15. A "know-it-all" attitude
16. Shyness or a withdrawn personality
17. Sexual aggressiveness inappropriate to the situation.
18. Inappropriate dress.
19. Unconcern for another's property or possessions
20. Dishonesty

After reading this chapter, you should have a reasonable picture of what *can* be done to effect more lasting relationships. Look for the obvious. Start a positive program of action. If you need support or help, that's okay. There is help available. I'm sure you have someone close to you (friend, employer, family member) who will stick by you and assist you in your new program.

You may want a professional's help. That's not a weakness on your part. You seek professional assistance in other areas. Why not the most important area—you?

I would strongly recommend getting into group therapy. Group therapy can enhance your social communication in the following ways:

1. Provide you with a positive-supportive environment.
2. Provide a definite time each week for social contact.
3. Provide supportive people who will be honest with you.
4. Help you see yourself as others see you.
5. Give you an opportunity to relate to others—their needs, problems, and victories.
6. Help you develop sensitivity for others.
7. Provide a situation in which you can build relationships.
8. Provide you with an intermediate situation between the way you are now and the way you wish to become.
9. Provide other people who will help you look at yourself and your problems objectively.
10. Experience the help of a competent therapist.

Besides group therapy, you should do some reading. There are some simple and extremely helpful books available. (A recommended book list is in the back of this book.) Read also for the purpose of building your vocabulary and knowing the current issues. This in itself will build your confidence and spark social communication. Any program of self-development that helps you feel good about yourself will also improve your social communication.

The Golden Chain

No chain is stronger than its weakest link! If we consider the elements of your life—your emotions, thoughts, experiences, etc.—what is your weakest link?

I can tell you mine. It is impatience. As I sit here on a sunny, somewhat smog-affected day, I am anxious. I want to say the right words to you. I want you to know my deepest thoughts. I want to establish a feeling of friendship and caring with you. However, I feel a sense of impatience—a grappling with words to convey me to you in the most sincere and honest manner.

Relationships do not always come easy. Sometimes there are many obstacles to overcome. For example, we all have fears of rejection, unreal expectations, or basic distrust. We evaluate each other by our past. Sometimes our experiences are not really reliable and can lead us into distorted or incorrect solutions. When we want to understand another person, we often judge him by our experiences with other people like him. This is dishonesty on our part. Let me explain.

What I am saying is that honesty—real honesty—builds real relationships. I emphasize "real honesty" to mean the type of honesty that comes from deep within you. Honesty can be fake.

Are there different kinds of honesty? Do we really need to be honest? What does it mean to be honest? Can we be honest with everyone?

Recently in our society, a specific and direct trend appears to be taking place. Honesty in some areas has almost become a cult. In our history, the image of an honest man has its place, such as George Washington's, "I cannot tell a lie," or Abe Lincoln walking miles to return six cents. These acts of honesty have become highly revered and furnish models to point people in a moral, ethical direction.

In understanding honesty, one thing needs to be clearly delineated—*Honesty is not a trait in and of itself. It must be related to a motive.*

I know a person whom I consider to be a basically honest man; however, he is friendless and alone. The motive of his honesty is to shock, embarrass, and even sometimes hurt people with his honesty. He might forcefully declare, "I don't like your new suit. It fits poorly." Perhaps he does feel this way, but what is his motive for saying so? I would suggest that his motive is to speak his thoughts, irrespective of the other person's feelings. His honesty, therefore, is not related to a need to communicate, but to a self-righteous need to declare that, "I am being honest in my feelings." Such honesty can sometimes hide some latent hostile feelings.

Another form of "destructive" honesty is when one has a secret sense of guilt and must tell the truth in order to be purged of his guilt, even though the telling of it may seriously injure another person. A case in point was of a friend of a man who had recently died. This friend knew a piece of unsavory information about the deceased. He could not refrain himself and told the dead man's wife about her husband. In a strange way, the friend felt relieved. Apparently his guilt was more important than the untarnished memory of his friend. His honesty was based on his need to experience release from his guilt.

Honesty for its own sake is a meaningless concept. One of the most important motivations for honesty is that it builds relationships. To be honest is to be lonely and isolated. I feel the bitterest moments of loneliness in my own life have come as a result of my failure to be truthful. When I am lonely, I cannot know the satisfaction of sharing—truly sharing with another person.

Honesty is a process of letting the other person know us as we think, feel, and live. The process is to strip away the illusions of roles and disguises and stand before the other person and ourselves as we really are. I have often felt, the more I know about other people, the more I am able to love them. This means knowing the bad as well as the good.

I have a friend who works in a psychiatric hospital of a prison. There, he met a young man named Terry, who was not yet twenty-two years old. He had red hair, a pleasing smile, and was quite shy. He had killed another person. Yes, he was a murderer. But my friend grew to care for him, because he was honest with him. Through their friendship, Terry learned to be repentent for his crime. Because they were honest with one another, they enjoyed a real relationship. The Bible tells us that we are all murderers if we hate our brothers. I sure am glad that God loved me when I was a murderer, for who hasn't hated at some time in his life?

Honesty, of course, builds trust. My husband and I have often said to our children, ''If you tell a lie, how can we know when to really believe you?''

Strangely enough, the converse is also true. Trust builds honesty. You probably find it difficult to lie to someone who really trusts you. However, the initial steps to trust are paved with honest communication.

It is amazing how much another person can be hurt once they trust you and then find out you have been dishonest with them. I know of a man who wanted people to trust him so much that he lied to promote it. Having people trust him was more important than actually having a relationship. It was only after a very painful exposure that he was able to learn the value of honest communication.

Trust can only be developed when we know that the other person is trying to be honest with us. Of course, sometimes we are unconsciously dishonest, but we do not blame another person for that. We evaluate him by his intentions, and not always the results.

Today, I have been reading some papers which I had asked my students to write for a course I teach. The assignment was to write about their lives—an autobiography. The students range in age from 18 to 21 years of age. As I read the accounts of their short lives, an insight emerged from the eighty or more papers I read. It is this: the students who indicated that their parents were loving and *honest* with them tended to like themselves in a healthy, constructive and productive way. The students who felt that their parents were dishonest with them tended to have a poor self-image. The students with a poor identity felt they had trouble being honest with themselves.

The process of honesty is also necessary in order to build a relationship with ourselves. Most of us never realize that we have to build a relationship with the person that we live every moment of our entire life with—ourself. Self-respect, self-image, self-confidence, and self-understanding are a few of the terms we use in reference to ourselves. We can criticize, punish, or reward the self.

The human personality contains several parts. There is the observing part of the ego which passes judgments, makes decisions, and moralizes about ourself. The practice of honesty with ourselves makes us consistent, open and true to ourselves.

Honesty builds the self. The motive for honesty is to enlarge our self-awareness, increase our confidence, and permits us a healthy form of self-love.

At this point some of you may say, "Yes, I know honesty builds relationships, gives us a good self-image and generally makes life better—but how do I become more honest?"

There is no magic formula for being a truly honest person. It is a process, a practice, and a way of life that we must aspire to achieve. The day you start to play the piano, tennis, or drive a car does not make you an expert. It takes time, courage, and a lot of hard work. Let me suggest some ways to practice:

1. Realize the necessity of honesty in communication with yourself, others, and God.

   You are a person with needs. You must meet these needs or you will suffer. It is as simple as that. These needs are for love, acceptance, dependence and expression. If any of these needs are not met, the consequences will be psychological symptoms such as depression, anxiety, physical complaints, etc.

   I know of a young lady with remarkable abilities. She is a sensitive, intelligent, and genteel person. But she basically dislikes herself and feels that she is at fault for almost all kinds of problems, which in reality are due to circumstances beyond herself. She is dishonest in her self-blaming attitude and cruel self-punishment. I find many people with this kind of difficulty.

   Lying is extensively covered in Scripture. There are many ways to lie. Blaming ourselves or others for our difficulties to excess are the two extremes. Actually, most situations we encounter in life can at least be partially corrected if we are honest in facing them.

2. Honesty involves risking.

   Suppose I reveal some truth about myself to you right now that could make me appear to be the kind of person you wouldn't like. I'm sure if you knew me, that there might be certain things that I might do that would cause us to disagree. The question comes to mind, "How much should I risk myself with you?" The moment that question comes to my thinking, the more I am restricted in my communication with you.

Frankly, I have very few secrets. Yes, I reserve the right to my privacy, but I have found that the more people are honest and risk themselves with me, the more I love them. If you tell me the truth about you, I have been given a precious gift. I will hold this gift in high esteem and guard it with all the loyalty and confidence I possess.

Honesty is a link in the golden chain of love. Love we must have, or our souls will suffer, wither, and die.

I know a young accountant, who was working with a firm that asked him to evaluate the total organizational procedure and find out how they could cut costs. After a great deal of analysis, he recommended that they let him go, since he had a high-paying executive position, and a person with lesser training could do his work. His firm took him up on it and let him go in a most unceremonious manner. Fortunately, he found another position, but he also won the love and respect of many people, including the author.

In marriage, love will not remain without honesty between the two partners. Love is like a fragile plant that must be watered tenderly. It thrives on honest communication. I have never seen a "happy" marriage based on dishonesty. People can learn to face almost anything if they are honest with each other. Love needs honesty in order to grow beyond mere attraction and physical stimulation.

We also need to practice honesty before God. In Psalms we see David pouring out his heart to God in his most humble manner. God honored him—in fact, David was called "the man after God's own heart." David was often wrong, but he was honest.

3. The practice of honesty is becoming vulnerable.

Perhaps this is the hardest. In becoming honest, we open ourselves to acceptance or rejection, friendship or alienation, warmth or rebuttal. Being vulnerable can mean being hurt—deeply hurt.

Some people have said, "If I never let people know me, I won't be hurt by them." The sad part of this is that they are hurting and lonely already, but they many times don't even realize it. Being vulnerable can make us susceptable to pain, but it also lowers the barriers to warmth, tenderness and caring. Is it worth the risk? I believe the answer is an undeniable "Yes!"

The opposite of honesty is lying. No matter how elegantly we enhance the truth, it is still a lie. Lying can become a way of life—a debilitating, destructive cancer that will corrupt even your most tender thoughts and feelings.

"Know the truth and the truth shall make you free."

The first beatitude tells us to become "poor in spirit." To me, this means to become defenseless before God—telling Him all about ourselves. He will honor this attitude.

In summary, honesty will help us:

1. Build relationships
2. Build ourself
3. Link us to love
4. Know God
5. Better communicate with God, others and ourself.
6. Realize that it is a Scriptural psychological principle.
7. Build trust
8. Understand reality
9. Be able to love more effectively
10. Obviously avoid lying

If you want a dynamic life, filled with excitement and love, be honest! Honesty always wins when it is related to the proper motives.

Communicating with the Opposite Sex

You are bewildered because you don't understand the opposite sex. You're convinced that everything would be okay if she or he were not so complicated. In the past few years, I have held several workshops on the subject. One obvious situation was apparent in each session. It was as though men came from another planet or women communicated with another dialect. Men and women arrived there convinced that it was impossible to understand the opposite sex.

Many communication problems can be eliminated by understanding the other sex. It really isn't such a monumental task. I think we could be safe in assuming that it's quite simple. By the term "simple," I mean that there is a definite line of demarcation between male and female. This distinction assists our understanding of the other and enhances our wisdom as we communicate.

Unnecessary diffusion of the sexes has caused stress and confusion. Uncertainty can be torment. I feel that there are many "displaced" persons running around today. The sad part of it all is that they are this way under the headlines of freedom and liberation.

Equality is not synonymous with uniformity. I think this is an extremely important point. Just because I'm equal with someone does not have to mean I'm like that person.

How many times have you heard such things as: "I'm no longer a woman—I'm a person." "Why do you have to see me as a man—I'm a human being." I realize that taken in context, such statements could make a valid point. Still, I'm afraid that they have concealed within them uncertainty and even possible calamity. Is it necessary to have an either/or situation? If I am to be equal with you, must I give up my own sex? Must I be like you? Must I act and feel like you? No!

Of course, a woman is a person with all rights and privileges as a member in the human race. And men are likewise persons with such inalienable rights. But, a woman is still a woman and a man still a man. To attempt a diffusion into some neuter-being is depriving all creation of its most potent motivation. Without roles, the stage is empty. Eliminate the flavors, and you decrease the appetite. If you refuse a male-female distinction, you are acquiescing to an unsavory life.

It is a biological fact that men and women are different. These differences do not have to complicate communication. They can, if rightly understood, cause a complementary effect on communication.

Within recent years, opportunities in leadership have opened up to women. I'm delighted with this progress. God gave me a brain and certain gifts and abilities. I'm thrilled that I can have an opportunity to use them. Occasionally, people try to corner me into an either/or situation. They do this by reflecting negatively upon my femininity, making jokes about my being female, or cutting down my leadership abilities. Their point always seems to be that for a female to be considered equal she must give up some of her female qualities. I find this to be a terribly illogical argument.

Recognizing the fact that there are different characteristics, we shall isolate them and attempt to close in the gap of understanding.

Let's Talk About Her

1. *Love*

A woman needs to be *loved*! Maybe I should repeat that sentence. A woman *needs* to be loved! An occasional whisper that you love her is not enough. Love to a woman is almost a spiritual experience ranging from intimacy to kindness to being appreciated. Love is small courtesies. Communication will break down if you fail to demonstrate a genuine respect for her image and needs. When you love her, say it and show it. This demonstration should be in the big ways and in the small—when you want to and when you don't.

2. *Little Things Mean A Lot*

Throughout the years, women have taken a great deal of static on being emotional. It's been an accepted fact since the beginning of time that women are emotional, irrational and hysterical. I have books in my library with chapters given over to proving the inability of women to cope with problems of leadership. These myths are finally being dealt with, but only because of the courage of both men and women to face the truth.

I hope one extreme doesn't lead to another. Just because we have overcome the irrational/hysterical image does not mean we want to become cold and aloof.

Men, you need to realize that little things mean a lot to women. Much of their emotional display will have this as its basis. Women are actually conditioned to this from early childhood. For example, a young lady is trained to notice spots that haven't been dusted. A mother's duties vary to the extent she's master of none. This learned response to details will obviously appear in other areas of ordinary living. It's not so bad when you think about it. If you want a woman who is efficient in attending to details, expect her also to require little things from you.

I've been trained to handle problems. The bigger the task the better I seem to perform. Still, if a loved one fails to notice my new hairstyle, or my birthday goes unnoticed it sends me to my room quite shattered. I remember one birthday when my family said to me, ''Tell us what you want to do tonight and we'll do it.'' Believe it or not, this statement sent me bursting into tears. The statement was made with the best of intentions, but it hurt me because I wanted someone to take out time to *plan* something for me. Do you see what I mean about details?

3. *A Woman Likes To Feel Feminine*

It's important for a woman to feel feminine. I didn't say that she needs to feel helpless—I said "feminine." Note that word, "Feel." I have heard so many women say to me, "I don't feel feminine." They usually proceed with, "I feel ugly and unappealing." After I question them a little, I find that what they're really saying to me is, "The man in my life doesn't treat me like a woman."

Let me go into some details on this. I usually find out later when interviewing her "man" that he actually does see her as attractive and feminine. In fact, he often reacts shocked when I reveal to him how his woman feels about herself. The following situations are common to these couples:

He doesn't tell her she is pretty.

He doesn't compliment her appearance.

He doesn't notice a new hairstyle or dress.

He doesn't recognize her feminine assets.

He doesn't appear to *need* her.

He refuses to say, "I need you."

He doesn't appear to be proud of her in public.

He won't spend money on her in ways that will make her more attractive.

He talks about other women to an excess—or compliments other women to her neglect.

He criticizes her abilities and judgments.

He doesn't show her respect.

He forces her to do work that is physically too hard for her.

He doesn't seem to want to protect her.

He ignores her when she is carrying heavy packages or struggling with a difficult task.

He neglects little courtesies such as: opening the car door, helping her to her seat, helping her across the street.

He is not warm and tender towards her.

He shows her little or no affection.

He screams at her or causes scenes.

He refuses to share in responsibilities such as: work, keeping up the house, caring for the children.

He never does "little things" that say, "I love you."

A couple came to me recently on the brink of breaking up. When I talked to the wife she said, "I never feel pretty or feminine around my husband. In fact, I don't feel like a woman when I'm with him." During my conversation with him, I heard, "I want a real woman. Someone who is soft and feminine and almost helpless." As the sessions continued, I learned that early in their marriage he began to leave more and more tasks up to her. She was a strong person physically and mentally so she quickly adjusted. She didn't rebel, and soon she was carrying groceries up three flights of stairs, painting the house and making minor repairs. He allowed her to do this for whatever his reasons and she let him get away with it.

Twenty years later he was paying for his creation. She was now self-sufficient and taking care of most of the chores (even those thought to be men's work). I pointed out these details to the couple and asked the husband for a description of what is feminine. I asked him to close his eyes and fantasize a feminine woman. He saw beauty, but he also saw tenderness, understanding, alertness and sex appeal. He came to the decision that femininity is all that it takes to balance out a man. He had forced her into being like him rather than complementing him.

Most of the qualities that he mentioned are innate in women. Men, if you want these qualities to show themselves, I would suggest you begin treating her like a woman.

The bed is *not* the place to begin. Too many women already feel that the sole reason for her being female is sex. Some women have never felt feminine outside of the bed. When the lights go out, after a hard day, she is suddenly supposed to feel like a woman. She doesn't! She feels like a machine. Treat her softly and tenderly the rest of the time and she *will* be the feminine person you want her to be.

Remember that word "feel." She may be feminine. She may look soft, and others may find her attractive. She, however, must personally *feel* that you think she possesses all these positive qualities.

4. A Woman Wants Security

Security is very precious to all of us. Insecurity, however, causes a great deal of stress on a woman. If there is a problem in her marriage, she is afraid of being left alone physically, mentally and economically. If her husband is gone on long business trips, she will often feel insecure about child rearing and discipline. When her husband ignores her or is cool sexually to her, she fears that she is losing her femininity. If a woman is in love with a man and there's a lot of empty spaces in their relationship, she will have doubts.

Financial security cannot be overlooked. There seems to be a strong emotional attachment to financial security with women. Children, home, furnishings and retirement all hinge on money. Thus, when the financial status of a family is threatened, a wife often feels that everything which is meaningful to her is likewise in danger.

A check list here might be helpful.

1. Do you tell her she's pretty?

2. Do you tell her you need her?

3. Do you show her you love her?

4. Do you show her you need her?

5. Do you withdraw from her when there's a problem or draw closer?

6. Are you honest with her?

7. Do you threaten to leave her when there's a problem?

8. Do you walk out on her during or after an argument?

9. Do you assure her that she's the only one?

10. Do you create empty spaces in your relationship?

5. *A Woman Needs To Find Her True Self*

The identity crisis is a fairly common phrase today. There's something to it that deserves mentioning. Regardless of how dedicated a woman may be to her family, she can't always be a shadow of someone else. She must recognize her own self and develop her own philosophies. I strongly believe that a woman who is happy and secure with her own self will be able to communicate better with the man in her life.

A man came to me for marriage counseling. The more he described his wife, the more I was sure she had no self-image. I suggested that she come in to talk with me. My initial program for her was a good long look at her assets and abilities. I suggested that he work with her on building her self-esteem. I shall never forget his reaction, "Won't that be dangerous?" I reminded him quickly that the present situation was already dangerous. It is always safe to restore another's self-esteem.

What About Him?

He needs assurance. A man needs your constant assurance that he is what you want and need. Call it the "male ego" if you wish; I call it assurance. Find his assets, and display your pleasure in them. Assure him of your love and satisfaction in every possible way that you can. Tell him that you love him until it finally becomes believable to him.

Let him have his pride. Take it away from him and you may have a monster on your hands.

1. Support Him

A man needs to know you are behind him and supporting him. In our society, it's extremely important that a man feel successful. Success, by my definition, is whatever an individual experiences as fulfillment. The last thing he needs is you pulling against him. There's a certain pressure in having to make a living and supporting the family. There's economic pressure with single men as well. A woman cannot remove completely the financial pressure, but she can add a supportive environment. This in itself will multiply his chances of success.

2. He Needs to Lead

A man has a strong need to exercise leadership. If a man is drawn to an aggressive, dominating woman, he probably has unhealthy reasons for it. In many cases, he has been dominated by his mother and wants to transfer this responsibility over to his wife.

When you have a serious relationship with a man, give him some room for leadership. Occasionally, you may even have to force his hand in leadership. It will pay off!

A woman in her middle years came in to see me. She was married to a man who had given over all responsibility to her. He was retired from work and made no gestures to aid her in household tasks. She was making the budget reach, doing the housework, cooking the meals and tending to other family needs. I remember her question, "Why can't he be a man and lead out in something?"

My advice to her after several sessions was, "Quit everything!" At least talk to him about quitting. Test him out. Perhaps the shock would twist his arm. The knowledge that this woman wanted a leader might be the key that would unlock his apathy.

3. He Doesn't Need Details

Try to keep his life simple. Most men are trained from early years to handle the big problems. The ultimate weight of responsibility for the family lies on the shoulders of the husband and father. Deep within every provider is the gut issue that he must keep the family ticking. This strain is often reflected in moods, quick temper and other annoying behavior.

With this in mind, make an attempt at keeping his life simple, comfortable and uncluttered with irrelevant decisions and problems. It is equally true that single men don't like hassles. Perhaps the quickest way to lose a man is to put a lot of problems on him. I've heard so many men say to me in my T. A. groups, "I really liked this girl, but she had too many problems."

4. He Needs to Protect You

In most men, there's a deep desire to watch over and

protect his woman. This is true whether she needs it or not. For that matter, most women have the need to be protected. I think that's terrific!

I sat in my office not too long ago with a woman who appeared to be strong and self-sufficient. She was having a lot of trouble in her marriage. I was amazed, however, when she confessed to me her need for protection. As the story unraveled, I learned that for years her husband had let her face the world on her own. It began with household tasks and progressed to making decisions on to earning the family money to almost total independence. Now, she was independent and doing an excellent job with it. She was personally craving for the watchful care and protection of her husband.

This is an unusual story in that most men look for opportunities to watch over the woman they love.

5. *A Man Wants to be Proud of You*

This may hurt, but it must be said. There is something in every man that makes him want to walk into a public gathering with a woman of whom he is proud. You may label this as male chauvinism. It may crush you to know that you are a symbol of his accomplishments. This may seem to you as though he is making you another symbol for his awards shelf.

Ladies, you might as well relax. You're wasting your time hurling accusations at the men. All the female liberation in the world will not change this urge within a man to be seen with a lovely woman. There are other qualities that will make him proud of you such as:

being well read, a good conversationalist, having a pleasant personality and a caring disposition. That's the way it is! There's no short cut and there's no rationalizing it away.

Why is it considered slavery by many feminists to be the best of what we are? If you are female, then for your sake—be the best that you can be.

Is It All That Simple?

Communication is never simple. In this area, as in all other areas of relationships, communication takes work. Perhaps I have made communication with the opposite sex sound simple. The rules are basic, but putting them into action takes a lot of desire and positive action.

My goal in this chapter has been for you to approach the opposite sex freely, honestly, and without feeling threatened. It is not impossible to communicate with the opposite sex. It is not impossible to understand the opposite sex.

We are living in a world where men and women have to study together, work together, relate to one another and live together. Many issues have been brought into the open with reference to the sexes—their differences, their sameness, and their difficulties.

Get acquainted with the opposite sex. Gather information. Information such as that contained in this particular chapter will make it easier for you to understand that person who seems so foreign to you. The knowledge of him, the knowledge of her reduces all the complications down to a beautiful, unique person who can compliment yourself.

Communicating with Your Spouse

What's in his head? I want to know.
What's he thinking? It doesn't show.
I'd like to talk, but I don't
Just because I know he won't!

Remember the scene in "Fiddler On The Roof" when Tevye says to his wife, "Do you love me?" She answers him by reviewing all she's done for him in 25 years. He persists by asking again and again, "But, do you love me?" It's apparent that in their culture, they seldom, if ever, discussed the subject.

A letter came to me from a woman several months ago stating that she and her husband had barely spoken to each other in ten years. She had been married thirty-five years, and considered him a total stranger. I have hundreds of letters like this one.

Make A Decision To Begin Talking

If you're only engaged, or a new bride, begin talking. If you've been married for fifty years, begin talking.

The decision to begin should be made NOW, and it should be a dual decision. Admitting your need to communicate is half the battle. Agreeing that it's time to get started is the next step. Making a clear-cut decision and commitment together puts you on your way.

Deciding What To Say

Most couples usually say to me, "What on earth do we have to talk about?" I know what they mean. So many years of silence have passed and now they have no mutual interests.

That's okay! Start talking about *anything*. Recognize that it's going to be a new experience, but also a rewarding one. The important issue is that you hear one another's voice and begin to share.

One quick way to begin talking is to find a common interest. It might be easier if it's something new to both of you—a new hobby, sport, books, plays. Setting a goal together will certainly give you something to talk about. Taking a class together will benefit you in many ways. Joining a club or church will bring you new experiences to share.

Give "Permission" To The Other To Communicate

Psychological permission is a unique part of communication. It will help speed communication.

What is involved in giving your spouse permission? "Permission" is saying the following things to your partner:

1. It's okay to talk to me.
2. It's okay to talk freely to me.
3. It's okay to express your feelings.
4. It's okay to be honest with me.
5. It's okay to be yourself.

We say these thoughts in many ways besides words. Making yourself available to the other spouse gives permission. With the busy schedules that most of us have, we need to take time out to sit down and talk. Pick out the best time for the two of you. It may be over coffee in the morning or after the kids are tucked in bed in the evening.

When your spouse expresses himself honestly, you reinforce permission by avoiding shocked reactions. If he expresses himself freely several times and in each incident you become hostile, he will probably refrain from honest communication. If your spouse tells you how he feels, don't proceed to tell him differently. Allow him to express his feelings.

I remember one couple that sat in my office begging for me to close the communication gap between them. As in so many cases, years had passed with little to no communication. In a desperate attempt to justify himself, the husband said, "I tried over and over to talk to her, but there was always a hassle. Our conversation always ended up in arguments at which time she would leave." He continued by telling me he'd rather have peace than communication. For his wife to give him permission to communicate, she will have to stop the uproar and scenes.

Build A Secure Environment

Security eliminates many fears that hinder communication. A secure environment has to be created. It takes work and time.

An engaged young lady told me that she was too frightened of her fiancee to communicate with him. I asked if he were physically abusive with her. She explained that whenever she disagreed with him or opposed him, he would leave. He would usually threaten to break up or to never come back. A huge risk was involved for her in honest communication. Rather than chance losing the man she loved, she would hide her feelings and swallow her words.

The following attitudes make up a secure environment:

1. I will always love you.
2. You don't have to agree with me.
3. I will never leave you.
4. We will always talk things out when there are difficulties.
5. I will give you the right to your feelings.
6. I will try to understand your feelings.
7. When there are problems, we will come together—not grow apart.
8. I will never threaten to leave you.
9. I will not bring up the past to hurt you.

10. I will not reject you sexually when you disagree with me.

Mutual Respect and Consideration

The old words of advice, "Treat your family like friends and your friends like family," are familiar to you. Simple words, yet they seem almost impossible to fulfill. Familiarity does lead to neglect, and very rapidly to disregard. More often than we would all like to admit, mutual respect and simple consideration are nonexistent in the confines of the family circle.

This simple piece of advice could save your marriage. And not heeding this advice is the easiest way to lose your marriage. *Show mutual respect and consideration to your family.* Because someone is "family," you assume that you can do anything in front of them, be any type of a person, say anything you want to and step over them. Not so! All of these small discourtesies will build up until you have a mountain of grievances that can't be climbed. The sad issue is that beneath this mountain lie small coals of fire which keep on simmering and waiting for their moment to erupt. You see the mountain, hear the thunder, smell the smoke, but you fail to see the base of the mountain.

You know some of the old tricks we use:

"He hurt me, so I'll get him later."

"She put me down in front of her friends—wait until I get her with my friends."

"He didn't like my dinner. I won't like him in bed tonight."

This stuff is dynamite. You can't win a game of insults. Defensive playing pays off. Stop the problem before it ever begins. Respect and consideration will do it.

This check list may help you evaluate your respect for others:

1. Am I as respectful to my spouse as I am to my friends, the people at the office and my business partners?

2. Am I as courteous to my mate as I am to my friends?

3. Do I consider the other's feelings?

4. Do I respect the privacy of the other?

5. Am I willing to listen to the other?

6. Do I respect my spouse's opinion even when I disagree?

7. Do I speak pleasantly around the house?

8. Do I use language, words and expressions that will build her up or tear her down?

9. Do I try to have an attractive appearance at home?

10. Do I have good health habits?

11. Do I have clean habits with reference to my room and my clothes?

12. Do I do my share of work or picking up so that no one person is overburdened?

13. Am I sensitive to the needs and feelings of every family member?

14. Do I use good self-control?

15. Do I do little things to make my mate happy?

The Golden Rule says it all: "Do unto others as you would have them do unto you." The word "others" applies to your spouse and your family. We tend to practice the Golden Rule in public and in business because it's necessary to get ahead in life.

It's far more important to get ahead with your wife. Here's a list of Don'ts which I compiled from my own counseling sessions:

1. Don't nag at your mate about something that can't be changed.

2. Don't put demands on your mate that would pressure him or her.

3. Don't criticize your spouse in public or in front of an outsider.

4. Don't cut down your mate in front of the children.

5. Don't bring up past failures and problems.

6. Don't interrupt your spouse while he or she is trying to express a point.

7. Don't belittle any work that they attempt to do.

8. Don't invade privacy.

9. Don't engage in name calling such as: stupid, jerk, dumb.

10. Don't make the other do all of your work for you.

11. Don't *cause* work for the other because you are too lazy to do it yourself.

12. Don't expect from others what you're not willing to do yourself.

13. Don't use your mate as a servant.

14. Don't develop obnoxious habits that will continuously repulse your spouse.

15. Don't turn the radio or T.V. channel without first asking the person who is involved in it.

16. Don't be difficult to look at or be around.

17. Don't be self-centered and selfish.

18. Don't lose control of your temper.

19. Don't ignore your spouse.

20. Don't be dishonest.

Words—Wonderful or Wicked?

Communication requires words. Words are important in your new venture, but there could be a problem. Let me explain. Regardless of your good intentions, you still have a vocabulary built over a period of a lifetime. You have verbal habits that may be hindering your communication. There's a possibility some phrases will have to go.

Words are powerful whether used negatively or positively. Through your words of encouragement and positive language, you give strength and courage. Words can be happy, encouraging, warm, kind, exciting, loving and unselfish.

On the other hand, they can be sad, negative, discouraging, cold, caustic, dull, selfish, crude, vulgar and hateful.

Take a quick look at your most recent words around the house. Into which category do they fall?

Words can be a habit as much as anything else in your life. You can get into the habit of being negative, yelling at people and being dull and selfish.

How are you coming across to your spouse? Does your

face show anger, hate, disgust? Does your conversation sting her with sarcasm? A woman sat in my office not too long ago crying over her marriage. Her husband was described as a dual-personality. Sometimes he was loving, caring, gentle and kind. At other times he was violent, full of rage and destructive. One observation remains strong with me from our conversation. She remembered very few words he used. Instead, she kept saying, "I can't stand what he's doing to himself." It was the anger on his face and the terror in his eyes that almost destroyed her.

I'm convinced almost anything can be said in the right way. By this, I mean anything can be said and accepted by your spouse if said properly.

Here's how it's done.

You eliminate the negative words. With sensitivity to your mate's needs and the situation, you present your feelings. The tone of your voice is mellow and warm. Your body language is open and caring. Your motive is loving and positive. The words are directed to a person who has your respect.

Attitudes Show Up

The way you talk and sound to people is affected by your attitude. Did you ever hear your wife say to the children, "Your dad's in a bad mood,"? What she means is that you have a lousy attitude. I realize attitudes can be momentary, but unfortunately, they often become a life's position. Imagine what that does to those around you? If it teaches everyone to do the same, your home will be a place to leave. Who would want to go home?

I remember counseling with a gentleman who had divorced his wife. He was reminiscing over the days of his married life. He recalled that on many occasions he would go out with "the boys" rather than going home after work. The verbal assaults were too much for him. Now, since his divorce, he looks forward to going home even though the house is empty. This is a sad story, but it brings to reality the unpleasant potency of words.

When you have a moment alone, lie down on the sofa and let your mind go a little. (1) Fantasize the scenes you have been in during the last year. (2) Fantasize yourself with your spouse. (3) Are the scenes pleasant or disturbing? (4) What are you feeling as the film rolls by in your mind (are you feeling happy, delighted, sad, disgusted, afraid, or sick)? (5) Do the same scenes keep cropping up? Is there a pattern?

Your fantasies will give you a fairly adequate idea of the words you are using and their effects. If you don't like what you see, let this be an impetus to construct a new vocabulary.

Let me help you by suggesting some negatives which you should strike off your list.

1. "I'll never be able to do that."

2. "Don't try that—what if you fail?"

3. "You haven't got a chance."

4. "How in the world do you expect to accomplish that?"

5. "I can't do that."

6. "That's too hard."

7. "That's an impossible situation."

8. "You've done it this time. You've ruined your chances forever."

9. "It's too late!"

10. "I'm too old."

There are words and phrases that break down another person's view of himself. Avoid using them:

1. Stupid

2. What a jerk!

3. How stupid can you be!

4. I'll have to do it myself in order to get it done.

5. You can't figure that out!

6. What a bum you are!

7. You're a no-good, lazy kid!

8. You'll never amount to anything the rate you're going.

9. Some "dingie" woman probably did it.

10. Use your head.

It's Not Always What You Say, But How You Say It

I'm sure that you have been in the company of people that seem to always offend you with what they say. Another person can be with you, say the identical same thing, but you feel comfortable with him. This is all part of communication.

Go back to your fantasies. The painful scenes could have occurred because of *how* you spoke rather than *what* you spoke.

Your attitude will come across in every conversation.

Your attitude toward your spouse will come through in your words, facial expressions and your hand and body gestures.

What goes into your mind affects what others see coming out of you. There are a number of ways your attitude can be damaged:

1. Are you around negative people?

2. What have you been feeding your mind?

3. Have you been wrapped up in your own problems?

4. Do you focus your thinking on good things in life or on your problems?

5. Are you unable to see yourself as good? Are others okay?

If you have the definite feeling that there is poor communication between you and your spouse, check out your attitude. When a couple comes to me, and I make this statement, one will usually begin by checking out the attitude of the other person. For this reason, I want to emphasize the words "your attitude."

Begin today checking out your personal attitude. I can assure you that if your attitude is correct, you will be taking a big step toward effective communication in your home. You may ask immediately, what do I mean by your attitude being correct. I think it's important that we define that word "correct." The word correct means that your attitude should be *congruent* with yourself.

Society provides many values, ideas and attitudes for us as individuals. Many of these are good. On the other hand, many of them can be devastating to us as individuals and family members. An attitude that is correct for you today may not be correct for you tomorrow. In one of my group sessions, one of the members asked me about my own personal attitudes toward myself. We were talking about congruency. He asked me if the attitudes and congruency that I experienced today would be the same that I would experience next year. My answer to him was simply this, ''I hope not.'' When I saw a few question marks on the faces of the group, I clarified my statement. I always hope today that I will be a different person tomorrow, and certainly a different person next year. My statement implies an element of growth. Growth should never end, and it is always my desire to experience growth from one day to the next—and certainly from one year to the next.

Now, let's get back to the correct attitude for you. What are some attitudes that play important roles in your own success and happiness as well as that of the other family members? I can only list the ones that have become significant to me in relating to so many people who have come to me with communication problems. They are: attitudes centering around self, trust, love, security, integrity, giving and caring, sex, finances, children, personality, individual growth, and religion.

In a marriage, you have two people who must form their own values, attitudes and philosophies apart from one another. Your question to me now is, ''But don't we grow together?'' Or you may be asking, ''When we marry, shouldn't we accept one another's attitudes, values and philosophies?'' I personally don't think that there is any information to back up the idea that two people must accept one another's attitudes, values and philosophies. I have found personally in my dealings with people, that the major problem is not that at all. On the contrary, people do seem to accept one another's attitudes, values and philosophies at marriage. The problem arises as the couple begins to grow. Through the growth process in their life, each individual begins forming thoughts of his own. This is okay. This is good. This is healthy. It becomes unhealthy, however, when the two individuals do not grow at the same rate, and do not give themselves permission to share their ideas with the other spouse. Equally essential, is the need to accept the values of the other person as he or she grows in life.

Let's suppose that you are saying right now to me, "I have a lousy attitude about myself, and I am ready to change." Usually when a person says this to me, they are willing to take a first step and that's exciting news for both partners and the counselor. I usually see in their faces and eyes, however, the idea that now the magic wand is going to be waved and all attitudes are going to be changed. This just does not happen. We hear a lot about positive thinking, and certainly all of us should try it and live it. However, it is virtually impossible to wake up one morning and change one's attitudes about such deep subjects that we have mentioned in our list.

We are in the here and now, but with us at this point in time have come all the events of our past. Yes, we are part of our unconscious that works with us 24 hours a day. We are what we are because of the people, places and things that have come into our life throughout the years that we have been here on earth. A blink of an eye, a change of mind, a new marriage partner, a large inheritance, or any other exciting event will not magically erase the past.

Am I suggesting to you that the past rules our life and we cannot change? Certainly not! On the contrary, we've said several times that we are to forget the past and start anew. I am building to a point that is extremely valuable if you want to effect change in your attitudes. The point is this: give yourself time, and get help in bringing forth this change. When I make this suggestion, I often get these words back at me, "Why can't I do it all by myself?" Perhaps you can, but it will be much faster and much more thorough if you go and get help.

Let me try to explain the total concept. Perhaps you have a negative attitude about yourself, and you find it virtually impossible to trust your wife, your children, or anyone else in your life. Because of your poor attitude and lack of trust, you have probably driven people out of your life. One by one you have seen people leave your life or hurt you in some way. As these events go by in your mind, you form the attitude that no one is sincere and no one is trustworthy. Further, the future events in your life, as well as the future challenges are dimmed because of the past failures. Now, you suddenly realize that your attitude needs to be changed. Making that decision is the first step, but it will not erase all of the hurt and anger that may be inside of you. A professional counselor or therapist can help you make decisions around every situation, and when you emerge from therapy, you will feel congruent with yourself.

Go back to our chapter on talking to yourself. Review the principles in that chapter. You are a very important person. When you become congruent with yourself, and you feel right about yourself, your attitudes will positively affect other people. I am not suggesting that at this point everyone will agree with your attitudes. Your spouse will probably not agree with every attitude, every philosophy, and every issue of your life. I doubt that you would even want him to. I am suggesting that if you know yourself, you have arrived at the proper attitudes for you, and you are at one with yourself. You will be happier, and will experience a security and peace that will positively influence those around you.

Coping with Controversy

There will be arguments in your marriage. Face it! It's totally unrealistic to believe that two people can live together for a lifetime without disagreeing. Personally, I would consider it boring to live without some conflict. However, many couples feel that controversy is bad and actually search for a matrimonial utopia. When they don't find this unrealistic bliss, they want out of the marriage. I've had women sob in my office over their failure as a wife. This sense of failure was based on a disagreement.

Since you know you will disagree, learn to do so agreeably. Since you know you will have moments of intense feeling, learn to deal with them and express them. Since you are confident you will get angry with your spouse, learn how to handle it.

It's perfectly all right to express your feelings. In fact, it's better to do so. If you repress your feelings, you're only buying time until an explosion. Your feelings will appear somehow and someway.

You and your spouse should make an agreement that it's permissible to talk about feelings when you have them. Each of you should allow the other the privilege of feelings.

I remember counseling a man who was separated from his wife. He wanted to reconcile the marriage. As we chatted, I realized that each time I questioned him on his wife's feelings, he would answer, "I don't know how she feels." I invited his wife in to see me, and she made similar responses. She finally confessed that she didn't know how she felt about anything. Since the beginning of their marriage, she had denied her feelings in order to keep peace. She had wanted to avoid hassles at any cost. Obviously, her husband had not given her permission to show any feelings. This resulted in her denial of all feelings, which was disastrous.

The remedy was not all that easy. Through private sessions, he had to deal with his own identity. Out of this effort came a new look at others. She had to learn to feel and to sift through her feelings. She also had to feel good enough about herself to express freely what was there. Together, they had to work at creating a secure environment for each other.

Express your feelings immediately if possible. Don't withdraw for long periods of silence. Avoid storing up negative feelings and grievances. Withdrawal and silence cut off communication and stifle your growth as a couple.

These words say all that needs to be said:

''When I do something right,
When I do something wrong,
When I push too hard or not hard enough,
When I expect too little or too much,
If I talk when I should be silent
Or if I'm silent when I should speak,
When I invert when I should assert,
If I try too hard . . .
Tell me!

I may not agree,
But I learn less and hurt more
by silent tolerance,
And I cannot correct that
Of which I am unaware.

On the other hand:

If you have a need I can meet,
If you have a space I can fill,
A curiosity I can satisfy,
A question I can answer . . .
Ask me.

I may not be able to help, but please,
Neither of us can grow unless you try me.
Don't protect or shield me
From the realities of yourself and your world.
If I need protection,
I will protect myself or ask your help.
And above all, remember:
I cherish two things, your love and honesty.
Having both is my deepest dream.
If you wish to join me in my dream —
Welcome, love.''

As you begin expressing yourself, eliminate the "you" statements. The word "you" is defensive and accusing. It's very easy to use the word "you" and put your spouse in a not okay position.

For example:
1. "*You* always want to argue!"
2. "*You* make me so angry!"
3. "*You* don't act like you love me."
4. "*You* don't do any housework."

Now, let's eliminate the "you" and change these statements around to a more positive "I" approach:
1. "I don't feel like arguing so much."
2. "I'm feeling a lot of anger right now."
3. "I'm not feeling any love from you."
4. "I think we should talk about how we can keep the house clean."

Can you see the difference? The feeling is expressed, and the problem brought out in discussion. The threat is removed.

The next step is to learn how to discuss and argue without tearing down one another's ego and character. The two of you should make an agreement now to eliminate name calling or any reflection on the other person or his character.

Here are some common phrases that completely demoralize one another:

1. "*You*'re really *stupid* for doing that!"

2. "That was a *dumb* thing to do."
3. "*You*'re a *liar*."
4. "*You*'re a *lazy bum*."
5. "*You*'re nothing but a tramp!"
6. "What kind of a *man* are you?"
7. "You can't do anything right!"
8. "If you have brains, they don't show."
9. "Why can't you be a lady?"
10. "You act like an animal."

You will also want to be careful not to bring up the past. There is no cure, and no future in looking back. It simply won't work to use the past as a club with which to play games and manipulate the situation. A man told me once that most women were hysterical at times, but that his wife was historical. By this he meant that she was always bringing up the past and his previous failings. This type of manipulation is unfair, immature, painful and disastrous.

If one party brings up the past to manipulate the behavior and emotions of the other, it's unsportsman-like conduct. The situation could always be reversed, in that there's no one without sin. With action such as this, you can easily see the pyramid of ill feelings that can build rapidly. Perhaps the person being manipulated has just been kind enough to express no discontent in the past for the other's unkindness! There can never be understanding and companionship when one party insists on bringing up the past. The so-called "guilty party" will always be at the mercy of the accuser.

Whenever the past is waved before the other partner, it is painful and many times even disastrous. If the party really has changed and asked forgiveness, further discussion of the problem only brings further grief and remorse. Repentance is certainly worthy as well as restoration, but too much of it is devastating and unproductive. A person can take only so much guilt and pain.

In my experience, I've noticed the following results from bringing up the past:

1. "What's the use—I'll never be forgiven."
2. "Sure, he's forgiven me—but it's not forgotten."
3. "I have no future because of my past."
4. "I'll have to acquiesce to her on every matter so she won't bring up the past."
5. "If they continue putting me down, I'll be as rotten as they expect me to be."

If you still have bad feelings about the past, it's time you resolve them. The old idea of forgiving but not forgetting may cost you a lot of life. I never cease to be amazed at the number of people who come to me with grievances going back five to ten years.

You can resolve the issues. Go to a professional counselor or psychologist and work it out. Many conflicts go unresolved because we choose not to resolve them. A certain amount of pleasure comes from hanging on to the old hurts. We have a lot of power over our mate when we hold onto the past. We don't like relinquishing this power. But we must if we're to grow.

Make Some Decisions About The Explosive Subjects.

Every couple has certain subjects that automatically cause an earthquake showing on the Richter scale. The more common ones are: sex, finances, family and in-laws, the working wife and religion. You probably have your own special earthquakes, I'm sure.

Come to a decision on them. See a marriage counselor and work through an agreeable compromise. Otherwise, you will go on year after year arguing over the same subjects, getting nowhere and playing all sorts of games to justify your side.

Some Ground Rules That Work

1. Allow yourself and your partner the pleasure of feeling.

2. Allow yourself and your partner the right to express your feelings.

3. Strike out the ''you'' statements.

4. Never name-call.

5. Never tear down verbally your partner's ego or character.

6. Never bring up the past in order to manipulate or win an argument.

7. Settle on the explosive subjects.

8. Don't postpone expressing your feelings for long periods.

9. Don't withdraw into silence and break off communication.

10. Stick to the *point* in your discussion.

11. Always look for a solution to your argument.

12. Let each person speak without interruption. Let them finish a point before you begin.

13. Attempt to feel what the other is feeling as well as yourself.

14. Listen to what the other is saying instead of preparing your case.

15. Never be violent or abusive.

16. Set aside time each week to sit down and talk freely about your needs and feelings. Don't let bad feelings pile up.

17. Learn to be honest providing your motive is love.

18. Don't play psychological games.

19. Don't continually yell and scream.

20. Don't walk out or threaten to terminate the relationship.

21. Don't stop until you come to an agreement satisfactory to both parties.

22. Don't withhold your love as a weapon.

23. Don't keep the argument running for weeks, months or years.

24. Don't carry your arguments to your friends and relatives.

25. Enjoy making up!

I want to give you some examples of effective and non-effective communication. These examples come from actual cases that have come to me over a period of years.

Example A:

You are tired physically, so it might be smart for the two of you to take off for a weekend and relax.

Wrong: "I'm tired! I can't keep up this pace. Something has got to give!"

Right: "I had a rough week, and I'm really feeling tired. How about bringing dinner into the den, and let's just relax tonight." (Later that evening you suggest a weekend holiday.)

In the wrong response, the husband states the problem of being tired. His statement, however, leaves the wife with a feeling of insecurity. She does not know if something deeper is troubling him, and she does not know what she can do to help.

In the right response, the husband states the problem of being tired, but he says that it is due to a hard day at work. He further invites his wife to share his problem with him. He is, in this way, expressing his need for her, and he is allowing her the opportunity to help him.

Example B:

You have had an extremely tiring day. You feel mentally exhausted.

Wrong: "Today was lousy! All kinds of things went wrong. I don't want to talk about it . . . just leave me alone and don't bug me!"

Right: "I'm tired and I had a hard day. I'm going to bed early tonight. Would you mind catching up on something that you've been wanting to

do? Maybe you can call Mary and the two of you can go to the show.''

In the wrong response, the husband does not give an indication of what the full problem is. The husband seems to be running away from any help or discussion. By a statement such as, ''Don't bug me,'' he is saying that he does not want to share his problem with his wife, and that he does not need her. He assumes that she is not entitled to the privilege of knowing what is wrong. He is giving the idea to her that if he did tell her what was wrong, she would not have the ability to help him. Lastly, he is being rude and inconsiderate to the one closest to him. If such an attitude occurs more often than not, it will turn her away from any concern for his well-being.

In the right response, the husband clearly states that it is just rest that he needs. He offers her an opportunity to do whatever she would like to do without him. He further gives her the assurance that he is all right.

Example C:

The husband has to be away from the home a great deal. Many things seem to go wrong. He calls and his wife begins to tell him all the problems. She expresses to him how much she misses and needs him.

Wrong: ''Look, you're a big girl now. I've got a lot bigger deal to worry about than all that stuff at home. You don't need me—you work it out yourself.''

Right: ''Honey, you do what you think is right, and I

know that you've got good judgment. Call me
here anytime you need me. Just remember,
I'm there with you even though I'm away. It
won't be long and we'll be together again.''

In the wrong response, the husband is openly saying
that his problems are greater, and that his job is more
important. Watch it! Be careful when you discredit the
work at home and the duties of the wife. If you do it
very often it will cause her to also become quite
disenchanted with being a woman and your wife. Such
responses will say to her that what she has been doing is
not important, and she will see other jobs which will
bring her greater recognition.

Also, the statement, ''You don't need me . . . .'' is
another little game. He is actually saying that he is not
needed or worth much and wants her to assure him that
she does.

The phrases, ''you're a big girl'' and ''work it out
yourself'' are cutting, sarcastic, and totally inappropriate
for good marriage relations.

In the right response, the husband is giving her the
security of being able to ask him for anything that she
thinks necessary. Still, he is giving her the ''go'' signal
to make all the needed decisions. He is practically
saying, ''I trust you, and I trust your judgment.'' Many
times in a marriage, the partners may be used to making
joint decisions. This is the way it should be. However, if
the husband is gone, the wife may not be confident in
herself to make quick moves. She may need that
assurance reflecting her husband's respect for her
leadership.

Example D:

The husband realizes that the family is getting behind in paying the bills.

Wrong: "You've been spending too much money and we're up to our ears in debt. Stop all the spending. I'll write the checks from now on."

Right: "We are getting a little ahead of ourselves financially so maybe we should sit down together and work out a new budget."

In the wrong response, the husband uses a move as old as the Garden of Eden. "*You're* spending too much money." Blaming someone else is the most primitive of all defenses. This type of attitude will bring frustration to your wife, and will eventually make you feel very unhappy with yourself. Learn to share the blame, and learn to speak those words, "I'm sorry."

He has put the entire problem on her shoulders, and in saying, "I'll write the checks," he is intimating that he is smart enough to solve the situation despite her guilt. He is demanding, and he is childishly scolding his marriage partner like he would a youngster. If you are familiar with Transactional Analysis, you would agree that his "parent" is showing in true and living color.

In the right response, we see an honest appraisal of a situation with a kind spirit of evaluation. He is saying "we" have a problem and together "we" will solve the problem. He is saying that he is just as responsible for the problem as she is, but in asking for her advice, he is letting her help him. This will assure her that she is an intricate part of the decision making, and further give her the security that honesty brings.

Example E:

The husband waits and does not tell his wife that there is a serious financial problem.

Wrong: "We're bankrupt. Now what am I going to do? If I didn't have you and those kids to worry about, I wouldn't have a trouble in the world."

Right: "Honey, we've misjudged some in our spending. We'll make it just fine, but we need to watch ourselves a little closer and pull in our belts a little."

In the wrong response, the husband once again "passes on the blame." It is the wife's fault, and it is also the children's fault. He waited too long to solve his problem, so in frustration he wants to run away. He cannot do so. He is verbally fleeing the problem by saying, "If I didn't have you and the kids . . . ." You can quickly see what this would do emotionally to the family. He is trying to cause them to feel guilt. He wants them to feel sorry for him. He is wrongly attempting to provoke some sort of help from them. This statement is egocentric and cruel. The family cannot help but be consumed with feelings of rejection and guilt.

In the right response, the husband is ready to share in the blame. He is sharing the problem with his wife, and he is allowing her the privilege to help with a solution.

Example F:

Your husband has been working overtime on two jobs. You haven't seen much of him for months.

Wrong: "You don't care anything about the family. If you loved us, you'd come home sometime."

Right: "We love and miss you. I think we'd all be willing to cut back on our budget so you could be home with us more."

Obviously, the husband *does* care or he wouldn't be working so hard. Her negative statements only add to his problems.

In the right response, her statements of love will encourage him, and the "permission" to drop off some overtime may be all he needs to take the step.

Example G:

Financially, you are in bad shape. There are also a lot of repairs needed around the house. Your husband has become apathetic.

Wrong: "We're going downhill. We have no money and the house is falling apart. If you were a man, you wouldn't let this happen."

Right: "I think we both realize we have some problems to face. Let's analyze what we can do about them and begin a program of action. The kids and I are willing to work with you on everything."

The first two sentences are most likely overstatements. We often make situations sound worse than they are. The last sentence is deadly. Question a man's masculinity and you've created a problem far worse than the original one.

In the right response, there is no denial of problems.

(The husband was probably trying to deny them through his apathy.) She simply provides support and hope for the future.

Example H:

A situation arises where you and your husband disagree violently on the issues. He forbids you to act upon a decision you have made.

Wrong: "You're not telling me what to do. I'll do what I want—when I want to do so. Try and stop me."

Right: "This decision is very important to me. I want you to listen and try to understand why I want to do this. At least, let's discuss the pros and cons and see if we can have a compromise."

In the wrong response, you are headed for trouble. By making a statement like "Try and stop me" you are encouraging your husband to do just that—and you probably will not like the consequences if he does. Also, by saying that he cannot tell you what to do, you are closing the doors to communication and not showing any respect for valid opinions that he may have.

In the right response, you are much more likely to have favorable results. The statements here show that you have respect for his opinions, and that will encourage him to consider yours as well.

Example I:

Your husband has developed a habit of not listening

to you. You are feeling discounted and rejected.

Wrong: "You never pay attention to me. You only care about yourself. I might as well be dead for all you care."

Right: "I really need to be with you and talk to you. Sometimes I feel like I'm not being heard. I need you and I need your attention."

In the wrong response, there are three overly dramatic statements. "You only care about yourself" is very damaging. "I might as well be dead" is throwing a lot of guilt over to the husband.

In the right response, she expresses her genuine needs. She also tells him that she needs him. This shows her vulnerability to him, and also gives him a "super stroke."

Communicating with Kids

Teaching Children to Communicate

Infants and children are sensitive, sensuous, and spontaneous. From the moment of birth, they express their needs. The responses they get from these early expressions become positive or negative influences to their future communication skills.

Communication begins at birth. It is at this moment that parents begin to teach their child to communicate.

Nothing Replaces Love

Convince your child that he is loved. It's not enough for you to know it. The child must believe it and experience it. In early infancy, this love is conveyed in ways more powerful than words. Holding, caressing and touching provide for the child's need to be nurtured and loved.

Somehow, when words become important to the child, parents forget the holding, caressing and touching. It's as though we parents feel the child can only communicate one way at a time. Words take over in the parent-child relationship, and sad to say, all physical affection is often left behind forever.

The love between you and your child must always be unconditional. I love you. I love you because you're you. I'll always love you. I love you—your good moments and your bad moments. I love your fears and your happiness. I love you when you succeed, and when you fail.

Unconditional love provides the security a child needs to experience open communication. This unconditional love is expressed at birth, and should continue throughout life.

I'm Glad You're Around

Perhaps the most fatal of all discounts is when parents say, "I wish you weren't here." Some actually say these exact words, others say so by actions.

Here are some ways you can convince your child he's not wanted:

1. Never being in the home.
2. Not meeting your child's needs.
3. Not holding or touching.
4. Physical abuse
5. Neglect
6. Body language that says, "Stay away."

7. Facial language that says, "I don't like you."
8. Leaving the child alone a lot.
9. Being unhappy over the sex of the child.
10. Acting out or saying the child is too much trouble.

I'm Glad You're You!

As a child begins to grow and communicate, he needs the assurance that he can be himself. This provides freedom for him to experience himself and express his feelings without fear of rejection. He begins his quest for identity in a secure place with the important people in his life—mother and father.

I'm sure you know someone who was rejected for their sex when young. Dad wanted a boy, but he got a girl. He nicknamed her a boy's name, dressed her in boy's clothes and had her on the ball field at three years of age. He's actually saying to her, "I'm *not* glad you're you. I wish you were a boy."

There are more subtle ways of doing this, but they are equally destructive: (1) the parent who continually makes fun of the child's clumsiness. (2) The mother who talks about her devil or monster. (3) The parent who stifles any show of creativity. (4) The father who will never answer the questions from a curious child. (5) The mother who rejects a lively, energetic child.

Provide A Supportive Environment

Children want to please the big people in their environment. They get their recognition from them. They are dependent upon them. For this reason, parents must continuously provide a supportive environment. If there is a defensive climate in the home, the child will clam up. A defensive climate will stifle honest communication.

Perhaps a description of a defensive climate would help you understand my point. Fear is apparent in a non-supportive climate. This would include: fear of rejection, fear of being alone, fear of punishment, fear of failure, fear of uproar, fear of physical abuse.

A young man who was in one of my T. A. groups related to all of us the defensive climate of his home when he was a boy. His father was very authoritative. There was always only one right way—his father's way! He told us how he would listen for his father's footsteps or for his voice. He learned to tell from a distance his father's moods. This gave him time to hide or run out the back door if the mood was a negative one. That's sad, but it's even more tragic to realize there is still to this day no communication between this father and son.

Critical and condemning attitudes are part of a defensive climate. A child should be taught to accept himself and others rather than criticizing and condemning. The critical attitude sets up many fears and defenses in the child. Can you relate to any of these?

1. Stay away from anyone who is different from you.

2. You don't belong with those kind of people.

3. If you don't take care of yourself, no one will.

4. You can't trust anyone.

5. Never talk to strangers.

6. Rich people don't care what happens to you.
7. Those people aren't good enough for you.
8. Can't you do anything right?
9. Why don't you get your facts straight?
10. You'll always be good for nothing!

A man in his late 20's came to me because of his inability to communicate. He wanted to talk to people, but when the opportunity came, he had nothing to say. When we looked into his childhood, he became uncomfortable with a discussion about his father. Finally, he confessed that he never talked with his father. He had tried to do so in his early years, but was unsuccessful. Every conversation ended in an argument. As the years passed by, the situation got worse. His father wouldn't allow him the courtesy of a few simple sentences. He was interested in his own ideas, and demanded absolute agreement from his son. The young man had concluded that communication was impossible. He projected these bad experiences with his dad into all social contacts. He would want to begin a conversation, but feared a repeat of all those hurts and failures in past communication.

Evaluation and accusing are part of a defensive climate. Instead of these, you should encourage problem-solving.

A young lad has seven minutes to catch his school bus. He can't find his socks. He asks mother to find them for him. In a defensive environment, mother would respond as such:

1. "If you would put your clothes away, you'd know where they are now."
2. "Why don't you clean your room occasionally?"
3. "How could I find them in all that junk?"

In a supportive environment, the mother might say:

1. "You look in that room and I'll look in here."
2. "Let's try to remember where you put them."
3. "I'll go look in the wash room, while you get your books."

Let me ask you—what possible good could come from the defensive environment described? While all of those accusations were being hurled, the clock was ticking away. The next problem the boy would be facing was missing school rather than finding socks.

Now, we'll begin with the particulars of teaching your children to communicate. Much of what has already been mentioned in previous chapters also applies to children.

Begin talking and don't stop for a lifetime. Keep the channels open. Talking keeps you understanding each other whereas withdrawal makes you strangers. There should be nothing too small or too great to be discussed with your child. As I write these words, I feel a sense of need to be so definite about this. When I think about my own three children, I'm so thrilled that we have grown to become friends. We have always been able to talk about everything, regardless of how painful the circumstance. Now that two of them are grown, we have become friends as well as family members. We're honest with one another, and we're comfortable in our honesty.

I feel so fortunate to be able to make statements like these. There are so few who are close to their kids.

A man said to me about a year ago, "I regret so much never knowing my father." I was shocked because I thought his father had only recently passed away. He continued with tears in his eyes to explain what he meant: "Dad and I never talked. The few times we did, there was a disagreement. As I grew older, I tried to get to know him, but he only related to me as a young boy. He wouldn't accept me as a man. He never knew me as a person. He didn't experience me as a friend."

Kids Are People, Too!

I can't tell you how many times I've wanted to stop a mother or father on the street, in the grocery store, at a restaurant and say, "Kids are people too!" Somehow, we actually get to believing that kids are sub-human. They don't get as tired as we do. Their hurts are not as painful as ours. Their disappointments are not as difficult as what we experience. A quarrel or rejection is easy on a child. Loneliness can be brushed off lightly. Embarrassment before others is nothing. Do you get what I'm saying? Each child is an individual with a personality and with feelings. That personality is meaningful to the person, and those feelings are intense.

I was rushing to catch a plane at the Los Angeles Airport and I saw a mother and father jerking and running with a little tot. His legs could go no faster. They were yelling and cursing at him. Finally, he stopped. He sat down on the floor and began to cry. They continued walking through the crowds, glancing back occasionally to yell at the child. He became frightened and his tears turned into hysteria. I was so angry, I could scarcely contain myself. I stooped down and tried to comfort the little boy. Finally, Dad came back to snatch him up. Not a word was said by either of us. If I had it to do over again, I would have reminded him, "Kids are people too!"

Remember the whole idea of respect in the chapter on "Communicating With Your Spouse"? That's basically what this is all about. Your child deserves respect. If you want him to respect you and others, teach him by your example. Respect begins in infancy and carries throughout adulthood. As a child grows in a wholesome environment, he will grow in self-respect and self-esteem.

Several months ago, I spoke at the winter conference for the National Educator's Fellowship at Arrowhead Springs. This is a national organization of Christian public school teachers. I sincerely wanted to share what I felt to be the greatest gift a teacher could give his students. The challenge of my talk was to produce in every student a good feeling about himself. This is basic. When a child grows in self-acceptance, he is far more able to grasp other concepts and skills.

On many occasions, you will disagree with your child. That's okay. There's nothing wrong with that. Begin with the fact that he is a person just like you. Realize that in proportion, his needs, problems and feelings are just as intense as yours.

If this is difficult for you, try your hand at fantasizing again. Rest for awhile and let your mind roll back to years gone by. See yourself at his age. Can you remember some of the super times and some of the rotten times? Of course you can. You're probably smiling by now because you see yourself in the same set of circumstances. It may all seem so incidental now, but when you look back carefully, you can remember the impact that some situation had on you. Don't stop with this one exercise. Keep it up. Probably one of the greatest techniques of understanding your youngster is simply reflecting on your own youth.

There have been times when my daughter and I were in total disagreement over a matter. The feelings were high, and both of us were almost desperate in our attempts to sway the other. I would somehow remember to look back at my life. This gave me time and courage to put myself in her place and try to feel what she was feeling. My courage gave her strength to understand my realm of experience. Our argument turned into sharing which resulted in mutual problem-solving. It works—believe me, it works!

Be Open And Honest

Share yourself with your children. Go back to our chapter on "Honesty." Review a little. Those same concepts apply also to your children. I'm not suggesting that you throw problems at them that they can't or shouldn't have to handle. I am suggesting that you share as much of yourself as possible with them. Will that be difficult at times? Yes, it will! Will that call for an apology at times? Certainly! Will you have to say, "I don't know" occasionally? Sure you will! Will you have to tell them you need them when you do? Yes, you will!

Nowhere in any parental guidebook does it say a parent is to be perfect, all-knowing and invincible. A child doesn't need that nor does he ever ask for that!

Often, at adolescence, the teenager is shocked to find out that mom and dad are imperfect. When parents go to great lengths to appear superhuman, the adolescent falls hard at the first sign of parental imperfection. Some of the most precious moments I've shared with my children have come after I have had to say, "Mom was very wrong today. I was tired and took it out on you. I'm very sorry, and I want to apologize."

Today, my children and I are very close. They are all extremely independent in all areas of life. I'm quite sure all of them could go around the world alone and do just fine. Still, the bond is so tight between us that I would trust them with my life. I'm convinced that all this is true primarly because we've always shared our needs. Ever since they were very small, I could present a need and one or all would roll up their sleeves and handle the situation.

For example:

"Mom is really tired tonight. I need your help around the house."

"Grandma is very sick. We need to take turns watching out for her."

"There's not much money this week. Let's decide how we can save."

I could go on and on, and I know you could prepare your own list. It's important that you be willing to be open to your child. He will learn to trust and share far quicker than if you shelter him from the reality of you and others around him.

Express Reasonable Expectations

Parents seem to vary from no expectations for their children to having excessive demands. Either extreme is confusing and dangerous.

You, as a parent, could provide all the materialistic needs of the child. You could be loving, generous and kind. Still, in your communication with him, you may express no *reasonable* expectations. Note the word reasonable. That's important! If there is no structure for accomplishments, no motivation, no goals set, and no challenges provided, technically, you're not doing anything wrong. But later in life, the youngster drifts because of a lack of structure. He is often confused and dissatisfied over his lack of accomplishments. There was a hunger for someone to expect something from him, and no one did.

On the other side of the coin, there is the parent who makes excessive demands on the child. This often grows out of needs not met in the mother or dad. Fathers often live vicariously through the son. This is seen in the dad who forces his son to play all sports because he was never able to do so. A mother who is left alone may smother her son to fulfill her needs of loneliness. Parents may have unrealistic dreams for the child's future. A particular college and a specific profession may already be settled on by the parents before the youngster reaches high school.

The pressure of these demands can cause emotional difficulty in the child. Should he face continual failure in his attempt to please his parents, he will quickly develop a poor self-image. Even if he can meet the demands, the majority of the time, guilt will bother him during the rough times. When the occasion comes for him to make up his own mind, he is too frightened and guilty to go against the wishes of his parents. He's cornered, and that's a terrible place to be.

Kids Can Spot Honesty

It's true that you can fool some of the people some of the time, but don't try to fool kids any of the time. It just doesn't work. A child can spot honesty. Yes, and a child can spot dishonesty. He knows when you're trying to pull something over on him. He's aware of your attempts to buy your way out of loving and caring. He's sensitive to your negative feelings about him. He doesn't want to hear praise that isn't deserved.

I taught in an exclusive, private high school in Florida for several years. The girls were from wealthy homes. Most of them had always attended private boarding schools. When the school year ended, they were sent to summer camp. I became very close to most of the girls. They were all alike. They all had wealth. But none of them had experienced love. Occasionally, we would have long chats together. I would ask them to describe what it's like to be so wealthy and have so much. Their answers would hurt me to the quick. "We're bought," they would tell me. They would explain by saying, "Our parents don't have time for us, so they try to buy us. That sorta eases their conscience when they only see us twice a year." One girl assured me, "Sure, I take their money and their gifts. Why not? I might as well get something out of them."

Of course, this example is an extreme case. Nevertheless, I think you can get my point and adapt it to your children. They want you and your love. They would rather have that than materialistic possessions. This is honesty, and this is what opens up communication with your kids.

There are other ways of being honest. To put it quite simply, tell the truth. The way some parents teach truth and live a lie confuses children.

Children are taught from year one to tell the truth. They are also warned not to steal. In most cases, it isn't long until the child realizes mom and dad don't practice what they preach. Little is said about it because children usually don't question authority figures. (That comes in adolescence.) They try not to think about it, but the inconsistencies definitely cause conflicts.

Two children came to me with a problem surrounding honesty. Their father had preached to them for years about the need for honesty as well as the evil effects of lying. They had been bitterly punished in past years when they had lied to him. Now, their father was insisting they lie for him about several business matters. He expected them to unquestionably perform for him. This is when they came to me. By the time they had made up their minds to talk to me, they were quite angry and bitter.

My advice was to go to Dad and be honest with him in a loving way. I suggested that they share their feelings of conflict with him. Fortunately, in this case, it worked and Dad saw what he expected of them. Lessons are learned by all.

Honesty is also displayed when you share your feelings. There's no rule that suggests that parents shouldn't have feelings. I firmly believe that the parent who is honest in sharing his feelings enhances free communication. It is honesty that allows for intimacy. When I'm not being honest, I'm playing a lot of psychological games. Games are played to avoid intimacy.

Here are some ways I've shared myself honestly with my children:

1. "I love you so much!"

2. "I'm so glad you're my child!"

3. "I'm not feeling well at all."

4. "I need your help today."

5. "I'm angry about what happened today."

6. "I'm so excited about our trip—I can hardly wait."

7. "I'm so sorry you're hurting. When you hurt, I hurt."

8. "I'm sorry about what I said. I was wrong."

9. "I'm proud of you."
10. "I need to be with you. I miss not sharing with you."

A few more helpful hints on honest communication would be:

1. If your child doesn't deserve a compliment on his work, don't give him one.
2. Don't say one thing and do another.
3. Don't give conflicting messages.
4. Don't give confusing messages.
5. Be consistent.

Effective communication is a learned process. It's your duty as a parent to create and cultivate in your child the desire and ability to express himself openly, honestly and intimately.

There are risks involved as in everything worthwhile. There will be times when you'll think it's useless. Don't give up, whatever you do. It's this open line of communication that will solve many problems, provide much pleasure and sustain your relationship.

Breaking the Communication Barrier with Teens

Is there a barrier between parents and teens? There certainly is, and it's a difficult one to break down. The barrier is put there by nature, and in some ways it serves an important purpose.

We'll discover the purpose as we look at some facts surrounding the adolescent years.

These are crazy years. The feelings are intense. The bad times are painful, and the good times are sheer ecstasy. Everything is topsy-turvy in the adolescent.

I want to review with you some facts concerning adolescence. These facts are often easy to forget when we get caught up in the drama of life.

Picture yourself throwing a large puzzle up in the air. the pieces go everywhere. You kneel down on the floor, gather up all the pieces, and begin the process of making a picture. It's never easy to fit all the pieces together.

This describes the adolescent years. The pieces of the individual are mixed up. The adolescent is searching for all sorts of answers. He's looking for all types of experiences. There are conflicts going on inside of him. His body has new feelings that range from delight to fear. There are other physical problems. With growth comes clumsiness and physical weakness. Bodily changes sometimes cause the teenager to look different. You will often hear a teenager say, "I'm ugly!", "I hate myself," or, "I can't stand the way I look."

The word "change" or "transition" is what adolescence is all about. This brings us back to my earlier statement: the barrier is put there by nature, and in some ways serves a purpose. Adolescence is moving from childhood to adulthood and that's a big step for anyone.

All those changes make up this transition period. Those changes must take place for adulthood to become a reality.

Naturally, change is difficult for anyone to handle. It's often quite frightening. Understand, however, that it's necessary and normal. How could we do without it? We enjoy the end results (maturity) but we hate living through the teenage years with them.

If you have an adolescent, you can count on the following description or a part thereof to fit him:

1. Growing fast
2. Not much energy (appears lazy)
3. Looks and acts awkward in early adolescence
4. Self-conscious

5. Strong desire for independence
6. Rigid—in thinking he is right
7. Rebellious to all authority
8. Self-centered
9. Wants *own* money and *own* telephone and *own* automobile
10. Aware and interested in sexual changes
11. Overly dramatic
12. Strong need for privacy
13. Strong peer pressure
14. Very emotional
15. Wants privacy

Does this description remind you of your teenager? I want you to realize that they're all alike! Some may be more obvious in these traits, but none are totally exempt.

But you say, "These characteristics are hard to live with!" I agree, and so does every other parent of teenagers. Still, what's the alternative? The transition must take place. Part of this period will no doubt be unpleasant. These characteristics will more than likely put up a communication barrier.

Am I suggesting the whole situation is hopeless? Definitely not. Start with these ideas and attitudes:

1. Every child must go through a transition period.
2. The adolescent years are as painful for him as for you.

3. It's nature's way of "breaking the apron string."
4. Every other parent is going through what you're experiencing in one form or another.
5. It will pass over.
6. Your child does care for you, even though he may not show it.
7. Expect communication to temporarily break down.
8. You are not a failure as a parent.
9. Your child will turn out okay even if there are rough adolescent years.
10. You are not being permanently rejected.

Does this make you feel better? It should—just knowing that your problem is shared by so many others is comforting.

I counsel teens and their parents every week. Invariably, the parents are convinced that:

1. Their problems are unique.
2. Their teen is the worst.
3. They are total failures.
4. Their child has rejected them.
5. All hope for the future is gone.

The look is always the same when I assure them this is just not the case. Their eyes, say, "You're kidding—that's hard to believe."

I don't believe there can be perfect communication between parent and teen. For that matter, I don't think it would eve be good or advisable. The transition must occur, and with it comes the restlessness and pains of growth.

The title of this chapter clues us in to what can be done. Our goal is *not* to establish complete communication. Rather, our aim is to break down obvious barriers. A secondary goal would be to relieve as much of the pain as possible.

Gain Some Information

Get some good books on the adolescent years. This would include: psychology books, books of development as well as many paperback books on teenagers and their problems. Attend seminars and workshops held to teach child development. The more you can understand your teenager and what is happening inside of him, the easier communication will be.

There is really no excuse for ignorance today. So often, parents will say to me, "But, I just don't understand my kid! He doesn't make any sense." After questioning the parent, I realize he doesn't understand the facts about adolescents.

If you've made similar statements, get some information quickly. It's easily available to you. Sometimes, we don't educate ourselves until a problem surfaces.

In my own work, I hold seminars and workshops all the time. I try to make them easily accessible and at convenient times. I've noticed a pattern which I think is quite significant. If I hold a seminar on self-development, marriage or communication with the opposite sex, there is a large crowd. When I hold similar studies on communicating with children or teens, the audience is small. What disturbs me is the reality that most of my work involves rehabilitating children and teens along with reconciling them with their parents. I'm convinced if parents would gain information early in child development, problems could be avoided.

What Were You Like?

Use your fantasy again. What were those teenage years like for you? Occasionally, when I ask this of a father, he replies, "Well, it sure wasn't like it is now. I didn't do all those crazy things." You may be thinking the same thing.

You probably didn't do the same crazy things, but you did do crazy things. You did have intense feelings. You wanted your independence, and in some way that was expressed.

Would you do this? Would you concentrate on your similarities? How is your teen like you when you were young? What part of you do you see in him? Did you ever feel like he feels? Did you make comments to your family like he's making now? Can you see and hear yourself in him?

This will help your communication. Your understanding is being increased and the solutions will come easier.

Be Available

Communication with an adolescent is like walking a

tightrope. You will want to be available, but not too pushy.

There's no need to talk a great deal. That's considered "too much" by teens. A lot of verbalizing is interpreted as lecture, sermonizing, and nagging. Much of what we parents would talk about is also thought to be boring.

Make it a practice to be around when you're needed. Once in a while, you could approach your teen and give him permission to talk. You may even want to express your need for a "rap session." Avoid an adolescent, and he feels alone and rejected. Excessive talking and attention smothers him. In quiet, subtle ways give him the confidence that you are there when there's a need.

Show Respect

We've already gone into the idea of respect in other chapters. With the adolescent, the concept is a little different. Before we discussed having respect for the individual. This would include: respect for his person, his character, his abilities and his rights as an individual. I believe we must add to that list when we talk about the teenager.

Respect his need for independence. Your child is *trying* to grow up. Nature is giving him a shove to help him accomplish the task. Respect his sudden need for independence. Begin treating him as an adult. Of course, you can't give him all the responsibilities of adulthood. He wouldn't want them. Remember, however, he's *not* a child. As he makes this dramatic change over, your respect and courtesies will smooth over many storms.

Not too long ago, some parents were expressing some anger over their teenager and his negative reactions to them. I gave them some information about his need for independence. Their answer to me was typical . . . "We'll respect him when he respects us." This sounded reasonable to them. I personally wasn't satisfied with this approach. I suggested to them that they start the ball rolling by expressing respect for him. I also suggested that they expect a reasonable amount of adult behavior from him. They were very hesitant, but finally agreed. We developed a program of action for them. Perhaps some of the suggestions will also help you:

1. Give a reasonable amount of independence.

2. Decide on what issues are of greatest importance to you. Zero in on these issues. Find out his feelings and work toward a compromise.

3. On minor issues, learn to look the other way. If you fuss and complain about all issues, you lose your potency on the major problem areas.

   For example: the issues most significant to me are: (1) honesty, (2) respect, (3) honest communication, (4) self-respect, (5) good self-image, (6) reasonable appearance and cleanliness, (7) driving skills, (8) moral judgment, (9) ability to love and care, (10) courtesy.

   In these areas, I am firm. I state my feelings and give reasons to back them up. I discuss all the above in great length with my teens. It isn't so difficult to do, if the same issues have been important throughout their childhood. I have found that if I press hard on these matters, the others fall into place. It's fairly easy for me to overlook faded jeans, long hair and a messy room when my teenager is honest, loving and has high self-esteem.

4. Spend time with your teen. Talk to him and find out what is high on his list of important issues. Generally, adolescents are sensitive to the following subjects:

    (a) friends
    (b) appearance
    (c) peer pressure
    (d) dress
    (e) school
    (f) money
    (g) room (privacy)
    (h) hair
    (i) sex
    (j) sports
    (k) automobile
    (l) driver's license
    (m) pets
    (n) alcohol and drugs

Stretch your thinking and patience as much as possible in these matters. Naturally, on matters such as alcohol, drugs, sex and the automobile, a great deal of information should be supplied. Any of these four could bring physical and emotional danger.

Remember that caring also provides instruction, structure, guidance and discipline.

5. Give your adolescent responsibility (enough to succeed, but not so much that failure is inevitable).

6. Give your adolescent privacy (no snooping through drawers and reading diaries).

7. Set boundaries that are reasonable and comfortable for you and the teenager.

8. Don't expose him to the problems of too much choice. Sometimes he wants your advice rather than your saying, "Do whatever you want."

9. Don't give him too many material items. Allow him the pleasure of appreciating the little things in life. Don't buy his love.

10. Give him the opportunity of building your trust. In other words, don't keep kicking him when he's down. Give him new chances to start over.

11. Express your needs and feelings to him.

12. Expect the same love, privacy and respect from him that you give to him.

13. Don't withdraw your love or threaten to do so.

14. Genuinely praise him.

15. Don't nag.

Loose Him and Let Him Go

Quote from: The Prophet, Kahlil Gibran

Your children are not your children.
They are the sons and daughters of Life's longing for
itself.
They come through you but not from you,
And though they are with you yet they belong not to
you.
You may give them your love but not your thoughts,
For they have their own thoughts.
You may house their bodies but not their souls,
For their souls dwell in the house of tomorrow,
which you cannot visit, not even in your dreams.
You may strive to be like them, but seek not to make
them like you.

In almost every workshop I conduct, someone will ask the question: "What is the greatest gift I can give my teenager?" Without exception, I reply, "Freedom." The responses are usually: (1) shock, (2) displeasure, (3) questioning. The question is always the same: "Why didn't you say love or God?" My answer remains the same—"Freedom".

The original question concerned the *teenager*, not the child. If the child has not experienced your love by adolescence, it will be very difficult to give him love at this stage of life.

God should have also been introduced at an early age. Am I suggesting that love and God are meaningless to the parents of adolescents? Certainly not! But, I am suggesting that these are more vital and potent in the early childhood years. Love, security, and God all provide the foundation for the storms of adolescence. Freedom allows for stretching, doubting, thinking and growing. I've seen it proven over and over that the parent who tightly squeezes the teenager, loses him. On the contrary, the parent who lets him fly away finds that he always returns home.

Communicating with God

We are all spiritual beings. I terribly resent being thought of as a purely physical being. There is so much more to me than what is merely physical. The same can be said for you. I have some very beautiful friends. They are beautiful to me because of the total quality of their soul and spirit. When we come together, there is a spiritual quality, a charisma, a spark that causes us to be warm in our relationships. I would call this "intimacy." Intimacy is a moment in time when two people meet mentally, physically or spiritually. When we have honest, open relationships with our friends, we will experience many moments of psychological intimacy. It is my belief that this is one of the evidences of our spiritual nature. Only man has this unique ability.

For this reason, communication with God has become a very important issue with me. I have shared with you some very difficult moments in my life. I have risked revealing so many unpleasant things about myself. I've shared with you my good moments and my bad moments. I did this because I feel it is terribly important to disclose myself to you, and with this disclosure, assure you that there is hope for you. I don't think it would be honest, however, for me to reveal all the not-so-good things and not share the beautiful moments.

When I was a very young girl, I was very interested in religious matters, and desperately wanted to attend church every Sunday. As I grew, I developed in my thinking processes, and began to inquire as to who God was and what His place was in my life. The minister of the church where I was attending was a very large, warm, fatherly type of man. I remember him being about 6' 5'', and he certainly appeared to be a giant to me. Once on Sunday morning, I wandered up to him, tugged on his pants (I was about knee high to him) and said these words: "I'd like to join the church." In a very kind and warm way, he took me to his office and began to explain a beautiful story to me. He suggested to me that I was a very important person to God, and that God loved me as an individual. He read from the Bible about God's love for me as an individual. As I reflect back on that moment, I don't remember all the words that were spoken, but I do remember one thing—the emphasis was put on the love of God. At that point in time, with a simple childlike faith, I thanked God for sending His Son in my behalf.

I grew up in the church, and throughout my life as a student, I became exceptionally familiar with the Word of God. By the time I graduated from high school, I had memorized gigantic portions of the Word of God and could possibly teach a class in almost any institution or church pertaining to Bible knowledge.

I had always surmised that God wanted to use me in a special way. For this reason, I went off to Bible College and majored in Bible and psychology. I never really lost my determination to do something for God.

With reference to my personal communication with God, let me refer back to that last paragraph. "I never really lost my determination to *do something for God.*" I was desperately lacking in that communication with God. I spent years and years studying about God and doing things for Him. I never experienced, however, relating to Him, talking with Him, and living with Him. My spirituality, my good feelings about God, my feelings about myself depended on what I was willing to do and what I did for God. Was I sincere? Most definitely. Was I informed in the areas of Christianity? Very much so. Did I live up to the standards which I had set for myself? For years and years, I very definitely did.

In the first chapter of my book, when I revealed so much to you about myself, you will remember how I told you that somehow I could not reach out to God during those dreadful years. I know now why I couldn't do so. I had really never reached out to God.

All these years, I had been in my parental ego state in my relationship with God. I had never been in my child ego state—feeling, loving, and reaching out spontaneously to one who was willing to be my friend and companion. Rather, I nurtured God. I know that sounds ridiculous. Who am I to make such a statement? And yet, how many others just like me go through a lifetime doing things for God and never relating to Him? I was actually trying to rescue God. I unconsciously must have felt that God desperately needed me to keep His work going. Thus, I remained busy—terribly busy working, accomplishing, and virtually trying to move heaven and earth.

When I was thrown into a crisis, and could not actively "work" for the Lord, I was at a loss. I had never experienced the Lord as a friend, and had never gone to Him as a child to a father. Of course, you can immediately see a further loss in this situation. I had only experienced His love as conditional. His love in relationship to me was conditioned upon my behavior, and my accomplishments. Never had I ever thought of a loving Father who loved me as I was. Where had I lost this idea of love? It had been so beautifully put to me as a little child by this minister. What had been said to me to make me turn so far from His love? I don't know how, when or where it happened. I only know it did. When I was so far from myself, so distant from the few who loved me, so hurt by the events of life, I also found myself cut off from a loving, heavenly Father.

When I finally decided that I had totally hit bottom, and when I further decided that I wanted to live, I remember asking God to show me that He loved me. This was the beginning of communication with God for me. From that moment on, I have never doubted God's love for me. Have people tried to get me to question

God's love? Thousands and thousands of times it seems people, friends, ministers, and teachers have consciously or unconsciously attempted to dissuade me from the love of God. You say, "But why would that happen?" I believe that the answer is so obvious. All of us have such tremendous egos that we want terribly to be needed by God. We want desperately for God to owe us a favor.

Since this event in my life, I have learned a powerful lesson: all God wants is for me to believe He loves me, and for me to love Him back. At this point, you might be crying, "Heresy." You might be thinking that what I am saying gives you a license to not do anything for God. Who have you ever known who has fallen deeply in love with an individual, and has not been willing to do anything or go anywhere for that person? I had been serving God out of duty. I had been striving for God in order to get a few strokes from Him. Since I have learned to accept His love for me, I have fallen more in love with Him. In this relationship, I now do far more than I ever did for Him.

I have said in almost every chapter that it is important to have information about the person with whom we wish to communicate. The Bible contains a great amount of information about God. We learn from the Word of God that He is all-knowing, omnipresent, loving and just. The scriptures tell us that God is Love, as well as Spirit, and that we must worship Him in spirit and in truth. All of these facts I knew, yet I was unable to communicate with God. I had been relatively convinced that knowledge about God would open doors to communication with Him. Yes, I needed the information. It was good to assimilate the facts. In the last few years, however, I have found that experiencing the Lord in my life has brought to life the reality of God. His love has comforted me, and His Spirit has guided me. When the facts seem dim and so far away, the experiences with Him remind me of His ever-present love and caring for me.

I believe our concept of God is extremely important as we approach Him in prayer. I have heard so often people say that they approach God expecting His condemnation. Many times we approach God with all sorts of fears. We have the fear of rejection, fear of revealing some of ourselves to Him, fear that He might not love us, or that His love is conditional, and the fear that we can never live up to His expectations for us.

As we have stated over and over in this book, how can we have an effective human relationship with another person if it is based on fears. Do you remember, in the second chapter, the many fears that are barriers to communication? Those same fears can become walls between you and your Lord. Now, when I approach the Lord, I communicate with Him as a loving Father and as a friend who knows me far better than I know myself. I approach Him positively, with the assurance that He wants what's best for me far more than even I do. I approach Him as His child. It isn't difficult for me to do this anymore because of the love that I have for my own children. I know with all the honesty I possess that my love for my children is unconditional. I know that when they are at odds with themselves or with me, or when they are in a not-okay position that I want them to come to me, not withdraw from me. I know that I have told them over and over again that we can work out anything if we are honest with one another. I know that I want to understand their hurts and pains, and that I can only understand them as I know what they are. I know that no sin could ever cause me to reject them. With this kind of assurance with reference to my own children, how could I expect less from my heavenly Father?

There's another barrier that has held back communication with God for so many people. Oftentimes, we think we have to be perfect in order to communicate with God. God only hears the prayers of a righteous person. So many times, people have said to me, "But I can't pray to God because I have been doing so many wrong things." At that point, my mind always runs back to the many times that I have told my children to come to me when they are in trouble. Is our heavenly Father any different? I hardly think so.

Then the verse is quoted: "The effectual fervent prayer of a righteous man availeth much." I'm so sure that that's correct. I'm sure that God honors the person whose life is committed to Him. But, I must ask myself more specifically, what is righteousness? From whom does righteousness come? What all is involved in that word righteousness? The more I study and experience life, the more I am aware that there is no righteousness in me. I am talking now about spiritual righteousness. God's Word specifically tells us how we receive righteousness. "And become one with Him, no longer counting on being saved by being good enough or by obeying God's laws, but by trusting Christ to save me; for God's way of making us right with himself depends on faith—counting on Christ alone.'' (Phil. 3:9, The Living Bible)

No where in the Word of God can I find any implications to verify that you and I have to be "righteous" in ourselves in order to have our prayers answered. To me, this is the biggest cop-out in the world. As long as I feel I have to arrive at some sort of standard of perfection, then I have all the responsibility toward a spiritual communication with the Lord.

In the last few years, I have been able to recognize in myself many needs. I have said to many of my friends that I am an extremely needy person. This has been wonderfully therapeutic to me. When I say that I am a needy person, I am also saying, "I need you." When I admit to my many needs, I must also reach out to God and tell Him that I need Him too. We do this with one another. We do it with our mates. We do it with our children. This is a relationship, this reaching out and touching is intimacy.

Finally, I would urge you to be honest with God. I think you will find as you peruse the scriptures that every person who was used greatly by God, was a very ordinary sort of person—an ordinary type of person in light of the fact that they had similar needs to you and me. They had problems, they had cares, and they had needs. The fact is, of course, that God does know everything about us anyway. But there is a therapeutic effect in being willing to open yourself up and express our true feelings honestly and openly to a God who cares. Honesty affects us. We are exhibiting trust in Him. We are holding out our hand in faith. We are virtually saying, "I believe in your love. I trust that you will never leave me no matter wht I tell you." That is the ultimate of communication.

I have stated on many occasions in this book that communication is a basis of all problems. Oftentimes, when I make this statement people will say to me, "Is not our spiritual status or relationship with God the basis of all problems or victories?"

Think with me for a moment. What is spirituality? What is a relationship with God? Aren't we correct in stating that a close relationship with God is based upon communication?

"If you live in Me—abide vitally united to me—and My words remain in you and continue to live in your hearts, ask whatever you will and it shall be done for you." John 15:7 (Amplified)

"But I will send you the Comforter—the Holy Spirit, the source of truth. He will come to you from the Father and will tell all about Me." John 15:26 (The Living Bible)

"If you want to know what God wants you to do, ask Him, and He will gladly tell you, for He is always ready to give a bountiful supply of wisdom to all who ask Him; He will not resent it. But when you ask Him, be sure that you really expect Him to tell you." James 1:5, 6a (The Living Bible)

God created man for fellowship. The need that moved the hand of God to create Eve was companionship. As I reflect on the definitions of communication from my experiences, I must conclude that God made me to communicate. That includes my giving to and receiving from God. My needs are met by Him and through Him as I meet other's needs. I experience Him through love, through trials, and through victories. His Spirit links with mine and I am aware that I am safe. His love causes me to love others. His tenderness teaches me to accept His long-suffering and mercy toward me. Communication with God is allowing Him to intrude into my thoughts and life. It is the ultimate of trust. It is the beginning of eternity.